10—

VILLAS OF THE VENETO

Joseph

These seem like your kind of house — somehow, I feel, you've just out of sight of the camera in these pictures

love Ben

Xmas 1988

VILLAS OF THE VENETO

Photographs by Reinhart Wolf
Text by Peter Lauritzen
Introduction by Sir Harold Acton

Harry N. Abrams, Inc., Publishers,
New York

Additional material translated by Graham Fawcett
Photography assistant: Kai-Christoph Tietz

Library of Congress Cataloging-in-Publication Data
Wolf, Reinhart, 1930–
    Villas of the Veneto/photographs by Reinhart Wolf; text by
Peter Lauritzen; introduction by Sir Harold Acton.
    p.   cm.
    Bibliography: p.
    ISBN 0-8109-1744-0
    1. Architecture, Domestic—Italy—Veneto. 2. Palladio, Andrea,
1508–1580—Criticism and interpretation. 3. Veneto (Italy)—
Description and travel.   I. Lauritzen, Peter, II. Title.
NA7594.W64   1988
728.8'4'09453—dc19   88–5877

Contents

Foreword   **7**
Introduction   **11**

Villa Foscari "La Malcontenta"   33
Villa Pisani "La Nazionale"   42
Villa Pisani "La Barbariga"   51
Villa Garzoni   54
Villa Contarini   58
Villa Emo Capodilista   64
Petrarch's House   70
Villa Emo, Rivella   74
Villa Barbarigo   78
Villa dei Vescovi   84
Villa Duodo Cini   90
Villa Giustinian   94
Villa Corner Fiammetta   96
Villa Cornaro   98
Villa Marcello   102
Villa Rinaldi   106
Villa Barbaro   114
Villa Emo, Fanzolo   126
La Rocca Pisana   134
Villa Capra "La Rotonda"   140
Villa Pisani   147
Villa Pojana   150
Villa Lampertico "La Deliziosa"   153
Villa-castle Grimani Marcello   156
Villa Godi   158
Villa da Porto Colleoni   166
Villa Della Torre   172
Villa Serego   174
Villa Allegri Arvedi   178
Villa Badoer   186

The villas   **189**
Bibliography   **200**

Foreword
by Sir Harold Acton

One of the most plausible chapters in Voltaire's satirical masterpiece *Candide* describes his ingenuous hero's visit to the Venetian Senator Pococurante's villa on the Brenta canal. "The gardens were laid out in elegant taste, and adorned with fine marble statues; his palace was built after the most approved rules of architecture." After his host had disparaged his fine collection of paintings, including a Raphael, his private orchestra, and the rare contents of his library, Candide exclaims: "what a prodigious genius is this Pococurante! nothing can please him."

"But do you not see," said his philosophical companion, "that he likewise dislikes all he possesses? It was an observation of Plato, long since, that those are not the best stomachs that reject, without distinction, all sorts of aliments."

... "but still there must certainly be a pleasure in criticising everything, and in perceiving faults where others think they see beauties."

... "that is ... there is a pleasure in having no pleasure."

Candide was published in 1759 when Venice was the leading pleasure resort of Europe. Venice and Carnival had become interchangeable terms. Travellers flocked there for the picturesque ceremony on Ascension Day, when the Doge symbolically married the sea, throwing a golden wedding ring from his superb galley into the waters, and pronouncing the words: "We wed you, o sea, as a sign of true and perpetual dominion."

But many patricians and wealthy merchants were as cloyed as Voltaire's Senator. Yearning for a change of scene on terra firma, they spent spring and autumn, if not summer when the lagoon was cooler than the mainland, on the banks of the Brenta or beyond, where they built country seats and planned gardens which have been compared with miniature versions of Versailles. Here such proud clans as the Marcello, the Corner, the Gradenigo, the Foscarini, and the Pisani would congregate with their courts of parasites and comedians to entertain them. Each family kept a houseboat called a *burchiello* to convey them by water as far as possible till they reached their destination, playing card games and gormandizing on the way. In the country they could ride, hunt, and cultivate their lands, or simply relax after the claustrophobic atmosphere of the capital. No doubt some of them shared the relief of Vernon Lee when she wrote: "Out of Venice at last! The wind stirs the sunburnt thistles on the rocks; the moving sunshine lights the first flame of yellow and russet on poplars and hedgerows; from unseen yards rise kindly farm noises. And the mists and languors and regrets and dreams of Venice are swept, are cleansed away, as by rain and wind, out of my soul!"

The long line of villas which follows the course of the Brenta to its outlet at Fusina was thronged by Venetian gentry till the middle of the nineteenth century but many of them have been abandoned and their gardens have vanished. In 1866 the American consul William D. Howells wrote scornfully of these "sad-coloured, weather-worn stucco hermitages, where the mutilated statues, swaggering above the gates, forlornly commemorate days when it was a far finer thing to be a noble than it is now. I say the villas look dreary and lonesome; what with their high garden walls, their long, low piles of stabling, and the passée indecency of their nymphs and fauns, foolishly strutting in the attitudes of the silly and sinful old Past, and it must be but a dull life that the proprietors lead there." Yet he conceded that there was "something very charming about the villas on the Brenta, with their gardens, and statues, and shaded walks. We went to see them one day early in October, and found them every one, when habitable, inhabited, and wearing a cheerful look, that made their proximity to Venice incredible ... I am not sure that I did not like better, however, the villas that were empty and ruinous, and the gardens that had run wild, and the statues that had lost legs and arms. Some of the ingenious proprietors had enterprisingly whitewashed their statues, and there was a horrible primness about certain of the well-kept gardens which offended me ..."

To visualize these country seats in their heyday you should consult Gianfrancesco Costa's album of etchings, *Le Delizie del Fiume Brenta*, published in 1750; several of Goldoni's light comedies evoke them at the same period, namely *Le Smanie della Villeggiatura, Le Avventure della Villeggiatura,* and *Il Ritorno della Villeggiatura,* a trilogy portraying the same characters in three stages, departure for the country, staying in the country, and going home. Most of his characters belong to the merchant class aping the aristocracy, or penniless nobles concealing poverty under ostentation. The parasitic guests criticize their hosts: one grumbles about the food, "quantities of meat but everything over- or under-cooked, too highly spiced. And how many birds were served at supper? Not more than eight, I'll wager. The fish was not bad, but what nasty oil it was drenched in!" Parties are discussed in detail and the dresses to be worn. "The main thing is to choose three colours that blend and suit one's complexion." Card games played an essential role: "in that house they are always ready to gamble at any hour. If only they played for small stakes, but no, it must be that wretched faro which is likely to ruin somebody or other." And the problem of arranging dinner tables was as acute as with modern hostesses. "A guest appears and says: 'Tonight I would like to sit next to So-and-so.' Another guest warns me: 'Mind you don't put me at the same table with So-and-so for I could not bear it.' It is indeed a puzzle to remember all the friendships and hostilities, and sometimes place the wife in one room and the husband in another." In one comedy a ruined nobleman repeats constantly to his steward, "Caro vecchio, fe vu" (Dear old fellow, manage it yourself), which illustrates the decay of his class in the eighteenth century: responsibilities were delegated to swindling agents. Yet many of the buildings, paintings and sculpture we value today belong to that frivolous age. Pietro Longhi (1702–62) illustrated the domestic scenes dramatized by Goldoni. As Berenson wrote of his pictures: "Everybody dresses, dances, makes bows, takes coffee, as if there were nothing else in the world that wanted doing. A tone of high courtesy, of great refinement, coupled with an all-pervading cheerfulness, distinguishes Longhi's pictures from the works of Hogarth, at once so brutal and so full of presage of change."

Even in the country social life was as nocturnal as in town: the more affluent began their day at about five o'clock in the afternoon and kept it up till four the following morning, flirting, gambling, making music, or strolling through the twilit garden. Their houses, cooled by the night air, were closed in the torrid daytime.

The patricians whose wealth had survived their ancient pedigrees led more strictly organized lives, even when a Casanova was lurking in the background. Perhaps it was in Francesco Morosini's villa at Dolo that Casanova first set eyes on the temperamental young

Anglo-Venetian Giustiniana Wynne. After his daring escape from the Piombi, the prison built immediately beneath the lead roof of the Doge's palace, Casanova met Giustiniana again in Paris and helped her to conceal a too carnal indiscretion, not without exploiting the situation to his advantage. Her mother's schemes to marry her to various rich old men having failed, she eventually married the Austrian ambassador to Venice, Count von Rosenberg, and presided over a literary salon. The charm of her conversation is reflected in her writings, such as her Pièces morales et sentimentales, and Ecrites à une compagne, sur les rivages de la Brenta dans l'Etat Venitien (London, 1785). Literature distracted her from gambling and consoled her of her amorous misfortunes. In middle age she befriended the wealthy young tourist William Beckford, for whom the palaces on the Brenta composed "a grand, though far from rural, prospect." Giustiniana Wynne was a pioneer of the numerous cosmopolitans who lived and loved in Venice and wrote about it, though there is a hidden irony in her Pièces morales. Later on Byron was to live with Countess Guiccioli at Mira on the Brenta. A villeggiatura at Villa Zola, where Marquis Albergati entertained his sixty or seventy guests, was thus described by a contemporary: "A scrupulous exactness in the preservation of order enhanced the splendour of the host and the magnificence of his palace. Punctually at nine o'clock in the morning a bell rang: this was the invitation to rise. There were two rooms where two barbers were in waiting to comb and shave the guests. The first to come was the first served... From the barber's room the guests proceeded to the coffee-room where a footman was always in attendance. When breakfast was finished and ten o'clock had struck another bell rang, which was the signal that the host had entered the coffee-room, where he held a private reception. All the guests went in to wish him good morning, and to consume a second breakfast with him. At eleven a bell summoned them to Mass and all the guests followed the marquis into church. After Mass it was delightful to see how many village maidens, neatly dressed, offered nosegays of flowers to their master, and were caressed by him and presented with a gift. Then back to the coffee-room, where some indulged in a modest game of cards while others enjoyed the swing or played billiards or withdrew to the study. At two o'clock another bell announced that soup was nearly ready, and the players invited each other to sit at table before a few more strokes summoned them to dinner. The dishes were so varied and delicate that it was difficult to make a choice. Serious talk was abandoned during the meal but not moderation: gaiety was mingled with good sense and sound morality. When the guests rose from the table the season determined what should follow. In summer some went off to sleep; others wandered through the garden till the bell summoned them to the grand promenade. In autumn this began immediately after dinner. Some went in carriages, some in sedans, some on horseback. Occasionally they would form a caravan: one took the kitchen pot in a bag, another the spit on his shoulder, another the polenta meal, another the water, another the wine, another the bird-snare – in short, each carried what was needed to cook and eat the polenta in the open country, and the food was seasoned with laughter and impromptu verse. Towards evening they would collect their chattels and go home to their assorted games. At two o'clock in the morning the party broke up and each retired to his chamber."

Goldoni had evoked the men and women who joined such pastoral excursions: their quips and frolics are sizzling in his comedies. At Villa Zola two broad staircases led from the entrance hall, one toward the bedrooms, the other to the top floor, so that after climbing two hundred steps you confronted a marble statue grinning at your discomfort. Practical jokes were generally appreciated, but they fell rather flat in retrospect. The amenities of villeggiatura, with its devices for time-killing and the transformation of night into day, must have been a mite monotonous.

Fortunately the villas on the Brenta, large and small, remain for us to populate the imagination, and there has been a recent trend of renewal in the Veneto since E. Landsberg, a devout Palladian, purchased and restored the Villa Foscari at Malcontenta, the first imposing palace on the canal, after leaving Venice. A perfectionist of relatively modest means, Landsberg even furnished the cellars and kitchens in traditional Venetian style and restored the frescoes by Giambattista Franco and Giambattista Zelotti which had suffered from centuries of neglect. Andrea Palladio designed this villa for Niccolò and Luigi Foscari in about 1560, and an inscription over the columned portico commemorates the visit of Henri III, king of France and Poland, in 1574. As Georgina Masson commented in 1959 in her Italian Villas and Palaces, the villa has probably exercised a more profound influence upon English, American and Russian domestic architecture than any other of the architect's creations, with the exception of the Rotonda and Palazzo Thiene. This dwarfs the neighbouring villas until we come to the grandiose Villa Pisani at Stra, built by Alvise Pisani when he was elected Doge of Venice in 1735.

The garden behind this vast edifice was converted into a park by Eugène de Beauharnais when he was Napoleon's viceroy in Italy, and Napoleon himself stayed there. The Palladian stables are like an equestrian chapel with a prancing steed above every Doric column in the aisles. The great ballroom was frescoed by Giambattista Tiepolo in 1767 with an exuberant Apotheosis of the House of Pisani, the last work executed by the artist in Italy before his departure to Spain, where he died. Obviously this was planned for the kind of princely pageantry seldom witnessed nowadays.

But the intrinsic charm of the typically Venetian country seats is equally apparent on a drive to Treviso and to Asolo beyond. Several villas that survived the Second World War are still owned by descendants of the families that built them, who farmed conscientiously and took Voltaire's advice to cultivate their gardens.

Palladio left his signature on the most sumptuous, such as Villa Barbaro at Maser and Villa Emo at Fanzolo, also notable for their interior decoration. At Maser we find Veronese in his happiest mood. His trompe l'œil figures in fresco – one of which is said to be a self-portrait, another of his mistress, the romantic landscapes with ruins, and the flourishing members of the Barbaro family with their pets on a balcony under a ceiling of Olympian gods – are among the most vivid images of the Venetian High Renaissance. Radiating health and sanity, they contradict the stale clichés about Renaissance corruption.

A path winding through the orchard beside the entrance leads to the circular chapel on the high road. Exquisite in proportion, embellished by Vittoria's statues, its effect is more pagan than Christian, based on the design of the Pantheon in Rome.

As a friend of Countess Marina Luling who restored the entire villa, I was often privileged to enjoy her warm hospitality, and each visit to Maser was an experience of soul expansion. One basked in what Berenson called "the frank and joyous worldliness" of Veronese's spirit, and the pleasure was enhanced by the violin concertos of Antonio Vivaldi performed by the Solisti Veneti. The music collaborated with the frescoes on the walls, accentuating their voluptuous flesh tones. Although Veronese and Vivaldi lived centuries apart, here they blended with the present and time was unforgettably forgotten while one listened. Vivacious lapdogs and a nearby aviary created a contrapuntal cacophony. Laughter and tears; arrivals and departures; there was hectic activity at intervals, and Venice was within a few hours' reach for those who wished to see the Biennale exhibition. But the dominant note was that of soothing serenity, with water trickling from the nymphaeum in the semicircular garden scooped from the hillside behind, guarded by male caryatids and winged angels, reputedly sculpted by a member of the Barbaro family. Here, too, concerts of chamber music were given on cool summer evenings.

At Maser one could imbibe the limpid atmosphere of a Venetian villeggiatura, which seemed to have changed little since the Barbaro brothers Daniele and Marc'Antonio engaged their friend Palladio to build it in the sixteenth century. The cheerful sound of human voices and footsteps was only interrupted by the telephone. Count Luling returned from his ride, and some of the house party rushed to welcome newly arrived guests in a shrill chorus which set the hounds barking. In the distance a church bell tolled the hour: another delightful day.

Although Henry James rebelled against Ruskin's didactic dogmatism, he granted grudgingly that San Giorgio Maggiore, for "an ugly Palladian church," (sic), had "a success beyond all reason." Goethe's taste was less prejudiced. In 1786 he wrote from Padua that he had picked up an edition of Palladio's I Quattro Libri dell'Architettura, "not indeed the original edition, which I saw at Vicenza . . . but a facsimile in copper, published at the expense of an excellent man named Smith, who was formerly the English consul at Venice. We must give the English this credit, that they have long known how to value what is good, and have a magnificent way of diffusing it." He described the bookshop as "a lounge for all the secular clergy, nobility, and artists connected with literature. One asks for a book, opens it and amuses oneself as one can. Thus I found a group of half a dozen, all of whom became attentive to me when I asked for the works of Palladio. While the shopkeeper searched for the volume they commended it . . . they were well acquainted with the work itself and with the author's merits. Taking me for an architect, they praised me for having recourse to this master in preference to all the rest, saying that he was of more practical utility than Vitruvius himself, since he had thoroughly studied the ancients and antiquity, and had sought to adapt the latter to the wants of our own times."

Apart from the conveniences of modern plumbing and electricity the requirements of our own times have scarcely changed since Goethe wrote, and the villas of the Veneto are supremely adaptable, as we find at Maser and Fanzolo. But here I shall not encroach on Peter Lauritzen's admirable text. As an enthusiastic resident of Venice he is more familiar with the Brenta suburb than most of us, and better qualified to introduce the architectural virtues of its palaces and villas than the blasé Senator Pococurante. His authoritative commentary, combined with Reinhart Wolf's magnificent photographs, have opened our eyes to that second golden age of the Venetian arts in the eighteenth century.

Harold Acton

Introduction
by Peter Lauritzen

The Italian villa reached a peak of perfection with Andrea Palladio's work in the Veneto in the sixteenth century. It was a height never since equalled or surpassed in the history of European architecture. Two hundred years later, eighteenth-century Englishmen were to spread the taste for his distinctive style of building to every corner of their vast overseas empire "on which the sun never set." Palladian villas sprang up in the English countryside and in the Carolina Low Country, in Ireland and Washington D.C., in Delhi and Singapore, in Nassau and Auckland, in Nairobi and Cairo, and in our own day a revived interest in Palladianism has produced a plethora of learned volumes and splendid exhibitions. Palladio has been described as the most widely influential architect the world has ever known.

But in order to appreciate fully the impact of Palladio's villa architecture on eighteenth-century Englishmen, it is important to understand the context in which Palladio worked. Because of his place in the sixteenth-century Veneto, it has often been said that if "Palladio had not existed, he would have had to be invented."

Palladio lived in what is now recognized as the great golden age of the Venetian Republic. Even the Venetians of the day realized that theirs was an exceptional era in the long history of an ancient and venerated political system. The splendour of their city and the work of their artists – men such as Bellini, Giorgione, Titian, Tintoretto and Veronese – seemed to reflect the power and prosperity of their thousand-year-old state.

According to sacrosanct tradition, Venice herself had been founded on the Rialtine Islands in the center of the Venetian lagoon on 24 March 421. Whether historians and scholars today would agree with the Venetians or not is beside the point. What is certain is that for the first thousand years of the Republic's existence, Venice owned hardly any territory at all on the Italian mainland. Her rich trade was seaborne and her vast empire spread overseas. And yet, as will become clear, the sixteenth-century Veneto farm villa and Palladio's role in perfecting it, was largely a Venetian phenomenon. Palladio himself was born in 1508, the son of Pietro della Gondola – a name that certainly suggests Venetian origins although he grew up in Padua. And the Padua of his childhood and youth belonged to and was governed by the city which the mainlanders referred to as *Il Dominante*.

Venetian domination in northeastern Italy created the context in which Palladio later worked. The entire century before Palladio's birth had been devoted to the creation of Venice's empire on the mainland, while the year after Palladio's birth, 1509, saw the destruction of everything the Venetians had built up and the *Dominante* herself on the brink of annihilation. Of course, this dramatic story reaches back farther in time, but in phases that can be usefully, if a trifle simplistically, summarized. The great moment of Venetian power and prestige overseas had come early in the thirteenth century, although her monopoly of maritime commerce in the eastern Mediterranean was already being challenged by the middle of that same century. The Genoese proved Venice's most determined and effective rivals.

Quarrels broke out in Levantine trading outposts and turned into armed skirmishes between galley fleets seeking to control shipping routes in the Mediterranean. The advantage fell first to the one and then to the other with intervals of armistice characterizing more

than a century of commercial rivalry between Genoa and Venice. By the later fourteenth century, Venetians were describing the increasingly bitter conflict as The Genoese War. The Genoese enjoyed one advantage throughout this long period: they found it fairly easy to enlist allies from among the principalities of northern Italy who, like them, envied and feared the wealth and power of the Serenissima. But despite this advantage and the very real successes of Genoese admirals in the late fourteenth century, the final victory went to the Venetians in the War of Chioggia in 1381.

Once they had triumphed over the Genoese, the Venetian government adopted an aggressive policy in northern Italy that was intended to secure the Republic against any future threat from the mainland. Venetian armies marched across northern Italy under a series of mercenary commanders and by the end of the second decade of the fifteenth century, Venice had conquered a mainland empire that extended westwards from the lagoon right to the gates of Milan. Of course this conquest brought Venice into direct conflict with the most powerful Italian principality, the Milanese duchy of the Viscontis and their successors the Sforzas, and would have provoked the hostility of the papacy as well had not the pope of the day, Eugenius IV, been a Venetian.

Just at this time Constantinople fell to the Turks and the Republic's policy of mainland expansion now began to seem a sound investment in more ways than one. Not only would it safeguard Venice's hitherto unprotected western flank, but it would also provide the Republic with land to cultivate for the foodstuffs previously brought to the island city from those parts of the eastern Mediterranean now threatened by Turkish aggression.

However, with Venetian expansionism over the Italian peninsula pushing back the borders of St. Peter's Patrimony, the papacy was bound to react, and in 1483 Pope Sisto IV della Rovere placed Venice under the church's Ban of Excommunication. This was the beginning of a chain of events which led directly to the greatest defeat ever suffered by the armies of the Venetian Republic. The fate of the Venetian army at Agnadello in 1509 was a foregone conclusion because Venice stood alone against the first great international coalition of arms in European history. What is still astonishing is that Venice's territorial ambitions could have aroused such a storm of reaction in Europe. The League of Cambrai had been organized by the Pope, who did have some legitimate territorial grievances to settle with the Venetians, but the rest of the coalition was really a triumph of papal propaganda combined with the greed of the individual participants. The eventual distribution of the spoils attracted to the Pope's side not only the Emperor but also the King of Spain, the King of France, the King of England and a host of minor Italian princelings. The Venetians certainly thought the end had come, not only for their mainland empire, but very probably for the Serenissima herself.

However, the Republic still had a secret weapon in her arsenal which she now deployed with utmost skill. She sent her wily and experienced ambassadors, famed as the most skilled in Europe, to the courts of each member of the League until she managed in a short time to turn the entire coalition on its head, manipulating the participants into declaring war on each other. The whole of this extraordinary tour de force was crowned by the Treaty of Noyon in 1516, with which Venice regained every inch of her lost mainland territories without a drop of blood being spilt on the battlefields of the Veneto. With the Treaty of Noyon the whole of Europe recognized the *de facto* existence of Venice's mainland empire. Thus the stage was set for the appearance of the Veneto's greatest gift to European culture in an architecture that could be conceived of only in peacetime. In 1516 Andrea Palladio was eight years old and was probably already familiar with his father's work as a stonecutter.

The period between the disaster at Agnadello and the Treaty of Noyon revealed an interesting aspect of the relationship that existed between the mainlanders and the government of the Dominante. Most of Venice's territories were being occupied by troops of the League, who believed the propaganda of their ally the Pope. They had been told that the Venetians were rapacious aggressors whose powerful armies had only recently conquered, subjugated and virtually enslaved the citizens of the mainland. They saw themselves as the liberators of towns like Padua, Verona and Vicenza. Thus they were taken unawares when more than one town rose up in rebellion against these harbingers of liberation from the supposedly oppressive tyranny of Venetian domination.

Another group of mainlanders fled the territory occupied by the imperial troops in search of sanctuary in Venice. These were the jews who arrived in the city in great numbers in 1516 and were assigned as their enclave an abandoned island called *il getto*, from the foundries once situated there. The tradition of sanctuary in Venice was an ancient one, beginning with the lagoon islands, which provided a refuge from the barbarian invasions of the Roman Empire in the fifth century, and continuing in the seventeenth century when Greeks fleeing from Turkish oppression settled in large numbers in the city.

In fact, in the very century when the Venetian armies were creating a mainland empire for the Venetians, the town of Salonika in Greece voluntarily submitted to Venetian protection and occupation. Of course, with their voluntary submission to Venice, the people of Salonika had calculated that the Venetians would help them to hold out against the increasing probability of imminent Turkish attack. But Venice also enjoyed a reputation for fairness and justice in the administration of the imperial possessions, whether they were overseas or close to home. One of the reasons for enlarging the Ducal Palace in the early fourteenth century had been to accommodate the number of tribunals needed to hear and judge the petitions and cases brought increasingly before Venetian courts by foreigners from the mainland. In addition to this reputation for fairness, the Venetians were known to grant a remarkably broad autonomy and independence to her colonial possessions. A governor might be sent out from the Dominante, but there was always room for a deliberative assembly made up of local worthies.

And it was to be these local nobles who, along with the richer Venetians, built the villas of the Veneto in the sixteenth century. Of course, villas had existed in the Veneto before the sixteenth century. However, none survive from before the late fourteenth century and the bulk of these rare early survivals can be dated from the fifteenth century when Venice was extending her sway over the mainland provinces. The reasons for the paucity of pre-sixteenth century villas are many and frequently help to explain the evolution of the Veneto villa. From the Pre-Alps to the River Po, the Veneto is a flat, fertile region crossed by numerous rivers and small streams flowing south to swell the Po or turning east to flow into the Adriatic. Many of these rivers would flood in the spring and autumn, making the land unsuitable for cultivation. A great deal of the villa building of the sixteenth century was as much associated with reclamation as it was with agriculture. Villas would have been relatively rare before extensive reclamation became feasible. Then, too, the flat openness of the territory, hardly broken or relieved at all by hilly contours, made the Veneto a perennial battlefield during the Middle Ages. The lords of Verona and Padua in particular, contested these lands among themselves. Later, their territorial ambitions brought them into conflict with the even more powerful lords of Milan or Mantua. The villa and its surrounding farmland can only prosper in peacetime. The architecture of the medieval Veneto was not the architecture of the villa, but rather the architecture of fortification. Numerous walled towns still survive to suggest the extent of the Della Scala or the Da Carrara or the Este dominion in this part of medieval Italy.

The Veneto was built over with castles more than villas. While the walled towns were fortified by the sovereign prince of a particular territory, the castle was often the stronghold of his vassal. And of course these minor nobles waxed stronger at the expense of the weaker rulers in a given dynasty. Some of the more powerful came to enjoy the privileges of investiture by the Emperor himself and became the sources of greatest resistance to the Venetian conquest of the mainland in the fifteenth century. Once Venice had successfully completed the conquest of these territories, she confiscated the lands of her enemies or her recalcitrant subjects and distributed them among the patriciate. Such was the case at Piazzola sul Brenta, where the fief of the Da Carrara lords of Padua was transferred to the Contarini family in 1413, or at Monselice where the Marcello family were assigned the lower castle at about the same time. However, over a hundred years later there were still quite a number of local nobles ruling vast territories from their castles. While they had acquiesced in the fifteenth century in Venice's conquest of the Veneto and had been allowed to keep their feudal estate, many of them changed their allegiances when the armies of the League of Cambrai invaded the country. To many of them the Emperor seemed a more suitable suzerain lord than a Republic of merchants and mariners, no matter how rich and powerful.

Once Venice had regained her mainland empire with the Treaty of Noyon, she moved swiftly and decisively to punish the treachery of her erstwhile subjects. Their lands were confiscated and either assigned or auctioned to trustworthy members of the Venetian patriciate. Thus the Pisani family acquired the vast estates of the Nogarola clan not far from Vicenza. But because the Serenissima always respected local traditions insofar as possible, the Pisani were actually invested with feudal powers at Bagnolo on behalf of the Republic. This meant that they would be both arbiters and dispensers of Venetian justice and law within their own domain. The Pisani saw to the dismantling of the Nogarola castle at Bagnolo and had it converted into an imposing villa designed by Andrea Palladio (1508–80). In so doing the Pisani were not only satisfying their own desire to have a country house built in the very latest style, but were also complying with a very specific directive of the Republic which ordered the castles of the mainland to be rendered defenseless by being converted into villas.

Thus, because of the constant strife and warfare and because much of the land was too marshy for cultivation, there were relatively few villas in the Veneto before the Treaty of Noyon. At the same time hardly any of the early castle architecture survives intact because the Republic ordered it to be dismantled. Even the defensive fortifications of some of the towns were purposefully breached although, since such communities would be governed by Venetians from within, the Republic could afford to leave a more substantial amount of these battlemented perimeters intact. The reasons for the survival of so few old buildings in the country lie ultimately in the peace and especially in the subsequent prosperity engendered by the Treaty of Noyon. Both the increasingly wealthier local landowners and the infinitely richer Venetian patricians simply tore down old buildings because they were out of fashion or else damaged or delapidated.

One castle does survive from an early period to illustrate many of the features characteristic of the richest country architecture as it existed in the fifteenth century. The original fortified precinct wall with its imposing battlemented towers has now disappeared at Thiene, but the original residence at the heart of the ward, today known as the Villa da Porto Colleoni, survives in its fifteenth-century outlines. However, there are two important considerations to be kept in mind throughout the description of this building and all the other buildings under discussion in this necessarily limited selection of Veneto villas. Firstly, to their owners, country villas in Italy were always less important than the family palace in the city. The land might have been the family's most valued possession, but the building erected on it was never the theater for splendid display that the town house became. Important architects were called to do their most carefully documented work in the city and not in the country. Palladio is, of course, the first to spring to mind as the exception to this rule, but even in his villa building certain conventions of decoration suitable to the country were respected in contrast to the way in which the noble landowner expected his palace in the city to be decorated. This is all by way of indicating how poorly documented these villas are. Documentation of the Veneto villa also suffered, like the villas themselves, from the constant sack and pillage inflicted on the country by invading armies and the troops of occupation, especially during the period of the League of Cambrai. Hardly any villa survives with its archives intact.

In returning to the castle at Thiene and the fifteenth-century villa/palace surviving at the heart of it, it is important to understand what kind of castle this might have been. Although the original fortifications have disappeared at Thiene, enough evidence exists to suggest their probable appearance and function. Two types of castle can be distinguished in the Veneto during the Middle Ages: the castle built on the slopes of a hilly site, such as the well-preserved examples built by the Della Scala lords of Verona at Soave or at Marostica. In both cases the steep site overlooking the town forces the building to be fairly compact even though long brick walls punctuated with impressive defense towers extend down the length of the hill to embrace and protect the buildings built on the plain below. The other type of fortification discernable in the medieval Veneto was designed for the flat land or the plain. This consisted of a tall battlemented wall completely surrounding the site. This kind

of castle incorporated a much larger open central space than did the hillside castle. Obviously it was easier to build on the flat than on a rocky precipitous site. Building material did not present a problem because, in both cases, the castles built in the Veneto in the Middle Ages were of brick. The walls of a fourteenth-century castle did not need to withstand heavy bombardment; indeed gunpowder was only just beginning to be used in siege warfare. Instead the castle walls had to be as tall as possible to deflect the missiles hurled and catapulted against the castle together with the thousands of arrows released by a hundred bows. The Della Scala were the great castle builders of the fourteenth-century Veneto and the tall brick walls of their many castles and fortifications are usually crowned with the swallow-tailed merlons which guide books claim represent their Ghibelline allegiance to the Emperor, as distinct from the square merlons on the castles of Guelphs who defended the policies of the papacy.

The finest and most elaborate example of a Della Scala castle built for the plain, and hence the one most useful as a prototype for the castle at Thiene, is the Castelvecchio at Verona. Here the walls enclose a very large area, in the midst of which stands a long two-storied building remarkably like a Venetian palace. The actual structure is an attempt to reconstruct the appearance of the Della Scala's residence inside the Castelvecchio, using materials and architectural elements found on the site. Nonetheless, the castle's fortification would have surrounded a large open space in which a palace-like building stood and this is the typology of the castle at Thiene.

In other words, the surviving fifteenth-century building at Thiene, known as the Villa da Porto Colleoni, is neither a villa nor a castle, but a palace once surrounded and defended by a long precinct of battlemented brick walls. The fact that the prototype of this building is to be found in the city and not in the country is an important clue to the evolution of the Veneto villa. Before examining this evolution in greater detail, it should be recalled that the Venetians dismantled much fortification and encouraged Venetian landowners to convert castle properties into villas. However, a kind of latent, if sporadic, nostalgia for the Middle Ages later resulted in the brief reappearance of castle architecture in the Veneto. An early example appeared at Roncade in the late sixteenth century. This kind of revival seems to have appealed particularly to families who enjoyed feudal rights over their lands rather than to the majority of Veneto landowners whose villas were the center of purely agricultural properties.

But the most important point to be stressed is that the Veneto villa type did not derive from the castle. This is evident if we compare the Veneto villa with that other most highly evolved Italian country house architecture: the villa in Tuscany. The Tuscan villa did derive primarily from the castle of medieval Tuscany and, like the castles they often replaced, the villas there were constructed of stone. Many of them even retained vestiges of defensive towers long after Renaissance architects had taken to remodelling them along Humanist lines. Most of all, Tuscan villas were built to enclose a courtyard – another vestige of their castle prototype – whereas the arcade or loggia embellishment of these courtyards ultimately derives from the monastic cloister rather than from the architecture of fortification. This embellishment of the courtyard also indicates an inward-looking orientation in the Tuscan villa. With only one exception – the Villa Garzoni designed by a Tuscan architect – out of the thousands of surviving examples, no Veneto villa has a courtyard. The only arcading will appear on the façade of the Veneto villa. This façade may be extended into an elongated rectangle while the Tuscan villa will keep the essentially square block configuration, again reflecting its castle prototype. When their respective interior layout is examined, the different evolution of the Tuscan and the Veneto villa types becomes even more marked. For example, many of the principal rooms of the Tuscan villa are located on the ground floor whereas in the Veneto these apartments are almost always situated on the *piano nobile*, the first floor above the ground floor.

The façade of the castle at Thiene, the Villa da Porto Colleoni, makes this clear with the fine fifteenth-century bank of Gothic windows located at the level of the *piano nobile*. These great windows with an arcade below on the ground floor suggest an architectural openness totally at variance with the traditional designation of the building as a castle. As has been suggested before, this villa/castello is neither one nor the other, but is in reality a palace transplanted from the city of Venice to the Veneto countryside. In his chapter "Gothic Palaces" in *The Stones of Venice*, John Ruskin described a progression of six arch types from the oldest twelfth-century survivals down to the sixth order whose point was crowned by a floreated finial, as on the façade of the Villa da Porto Colleoni at Thiene. The sixth order of window arch makes its appearance in Venetian Gothic architecture in the second half of the fifteenth century – and then disappears altogether with the abandonment of Gothic decoration in favour of Renaissance motifs by around 1475–80. If this detail gives us a date for part of this villa's façade, the overall shape and appearance of the building suggests an even older prototype.

Architectural historians usually describe this prototype as a Veneto-Byzantine palace and point to the building constructed on the Grand Canal in 1225 for Matteo Palmieri as the most complete example of the style surviving in Venice. Today this palace is known as the Fondaco dei Turchi from its use as an emporium and residence of the Turkish merchants living in Venice. Its current appearance is the result of radical restoration work carried out a little over a century ago. Although the aesthetic criteria used in this operation were unsatisfactory, at least we have a fairly accurate reconstruction of an early palace type based on the survival of much of the original structure. The Veneto-Byzantine palace façade was characterized by a long arcade on the ground floor of the waterfront façade with another series of openings forming a loggia on the floor above. The central block of this remarkably open architecture was then flanked by taller towers at either end. Without speculating about the internal arrangement of the Fondaco dei Turchi, the similarity with the Villa da Porto Colleoni façade is obvious. Although we are only given a glimpse of its appearance in documents and in the building that eventually replaced it, there was an even more important prototype for this kind of building in Venice . This was the second version of the Doge's Palace, built by the great Doge Sebastiano Ziani late in the 1170s. The two levels of arcading and the flanking towers of Ziani's ducal palace were eventually incorporated in the Gothic architecture of the third and

final version of the palace built on the waterfront in 1340. The prestige of Ziani's Veneto-Byzantine style building would have recommended it as a prototype for buildings everywhere, especially during the centuries when Venice's reputation for justice, power and wealth began to spread to the mainland.

Scholars and architectural historians have often speculated on the source of this style of so-called Veneto-Byzantine building which appears to be unique to Venice. These buildings were remarkable for being so very open at a time when siege warfare, fortified tower houses or castles were the norm elsewhere in Italy. But of course Venice had no need of such protection. The lagoon was her defense, the sacred walls of the Patria, *sacros muros patrie* in the words of the sixteenth-century Latin inscription. Unfortunately, not enough authentic early Byzantine domestic architecture survives to permit more than the general supposition that this type of building originated in Constantinople. One has to delve deeper into the past to find the source of Venice's Veneto-Byzantine palaces. Ironically enough for our purposes, a fairly likely candidate exists in a Roman villa built for the Emperor Diocletian on the shores of the Adriatic. The imperial villa of Spalato, (Split) in today's Yugoslavia, would have been familiar to the earliest Venetian merchants and would have later provided a suitably impressive model for the richest of them who wished to build the grandest possible town house in Venice. The façade of Diocletian's villa had a long ground floor arcade on the water's edge with an upper floor equally open with arcading. In addition, either end of this lengthy prospect was flanked by towers. Although Diocletian's sea front crypto-porticus was exceptionally long, even by Venetian standards, its general disposition corresponds to other Roman villas whose appearance survives only in Roman mosaic floors, such as the famous fragments displayed in Carthage's Bardo Museum. But the Venetians of Sebastiano Ziani's era or even Matteo Palmieri's later generation may well have known examples of such villas in North Africa and elsewhere that disappeared only subsequently.

Whatever the relevance of this speculation, it serves to introduce the often corroborated fact that the villas of the Veneto, no matter when they were built or by whom, evolved from the urban domestic architecture of Venice. The Villa/castello da Porto Colleoni at Thiene proves this correlation in more ways than one. In Venice the palace was a compact block. Building space on the hundred or more islands of the city was always at a premium but especially during the Middle Ages when Venice's population rose to 200,000 at a time when Paris had only 40,000 inhabitants, London half that number and Rome only 15,000. The Venetian palace never wasted space on internal courtyards, meandering wings or ornamental porticos. In the country, where there were no limitations of space, villa builders could have indulged in any such whims and extravagances. The fact that they did not is further confirmation of the importance of the Venetian palace prototype.

This economy of space appears in another detail of the Venetian palace where even the grandest lacks the kind of monumental staircase that became characteristic of rich town houses throughout Europe. And again, in the country even the most lavish of Palladio's plans have little more than a narrow spiral staircase tucked away in a corner of the house to provide access to the upper floors. The *piano nobile* of many of Palladio's villas was reached by an outside front staircase that arrived under a temple front portico, as we shall see, but the mere fact that the villa's main rooms were located on the *piano nobile* and not on the ground floor was yet another convention borrowed from the Venetian palace.

In Venice the ground floor was never suitable for such rooms because the palace was often built directly on the mud flat. It is true that by Palladio's day many mainland villas were built on reclaimed marshland sites, but long before the mid sixteenth century the principal living floor of the Veneto villas was the *piano nobile*. It was only in the eighteenth century that the Veneto villa began to incorporate a central hall located on the ground floor, but that was true only in cases where an exaggerated height was used to spectacular effect and the hall actually rose through two full floors of the building.

The central hall in a mainland villa was yet another derivation from the palace building practice of Venice. In Venice the upper and lower floor arcades on the waterfront façade of Veneto-Byzantine palaces such as the Fondaco dei Turchi underwent a transformation in the Gothic period. The lower arcade was reduced in breadth, usually to three arches, or else became only a single pointed arch watergate entrance. The upper arcade of loggia was also diminished although it always remained wider than the ground floor openings. On the other hand the flanking towers were now a more substantial part of a façade which could be described as divided into three distinct sections. The central bank of windows on the *piano nobile* remained a characteristic feature of Venetian palace architecture and decoration through the four remaining centuries of the Republic's existence. All Venetian Gothic, Venetian Renaissance, Venetian Baroque and Venetian neo-Classical palaces are distinguished by the presence of these windows in the center of their façades.

This was not a purely decorative device, but provided the light for an immensely deep central hall that ran the entire depth of the palace or *piano nobile*. This hall, known as the *portego*, and really a gallery/corridor located at the heart of the house, was also illuminated by an identical bank of windows on the land side. Again this feature of palace building in Venice was determined by the exigencies of the site where crowded building eliminated the possibility of lighting this hall from the sides. The curious fact is that on the mainland, where space was no problem, an identical *sala del portego* was the center of the villa throughout the Gothic, Renaissance, Baroque and neo-Classical periods. And to make the point even clearer, this distinctively long gallery/corridor is not to be found in the palaces or villas of either Rome or Florence at this or at any subsequent time.

The conventions of palace construction in Venice influence other aspects of villa building as well. Building on mud flats required the use of the lightest possible building materials and so the standard repertoire of Venetian building included brick, wood and stucco, but generally excluded stone, save for decorative facing or architectural accents. This was even more true in the country. Palladio's masterworks, often copied in stone on a grandiose scale by eighteenth-century Englishmen, were always built of brick and stucco. Only one of his villas, built for the Serego family at Santa Sofia near Verona, is made of stone. The columns of the temple front porticos of the Villa Emo at Fanzolo or the famous Villa

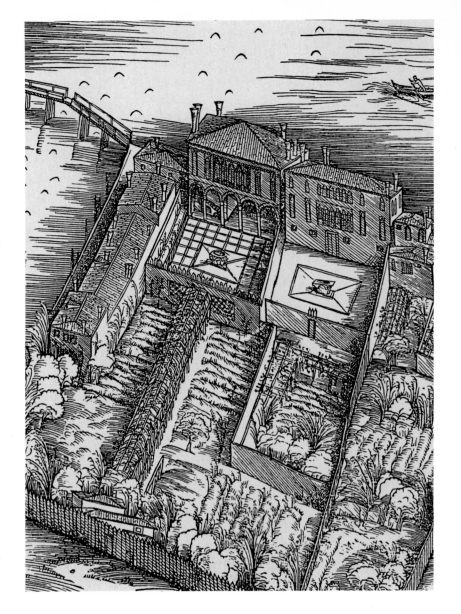

Foscari at Malcontenta reveal their rich red colour. The red brick still shows through at Thiene where the old-fashioned towers rise high above the roof at either end of the long rectangular façade. As happened in Venice's palaces, these anachronistic towers were suppressed in mainland villa architecture and the whole breadth of the building was covered by one shallow pitched roof. However, here too a distinctively Venetian feature of domestic architecture reveals itself. Venetian law forbade the use of overhanging eaves in the city because such a feature would have darkened the narrow *calle* excessively. But why not use them in the country? They are certainly a distinctive feature of most Quattro- and Cinquecento Tuscan villas. Once again, the answer may be one of convention, or of a pervasive aesthetic inclination.

The villas were not built by Venetians alone. In fact, of the literally thousands that survive in today's Veneto region only a fraction were built by the Dominante's native families. The far greater majority were designed for local landowners whose ancestors came from Padua, Treviso, Vicenza, Verona, Bergamo or Brescia. It is for this reason that I do not believe that a book devoted to the study of these villas should ever be called, as has recently happened, *Venetian Villas*. They were Veneto villas no matter where the inspiration for them may have originated. However, it was the power and prestige of Venetian culture and the fact that even in the

Villa with garden on the Giudecca, Venice,
detail from the woodcut of an aerial view of Venice, 1500,
by Jacopo de'Barbari (Museo Correr, Venice).

fifteenth century Venice was widely recognized as architecturally the richest city in Europe, that made her palaces the models for the palaces of the mainland towns as well as the models for the villas of the surrounding countryside.

If Venice's Veneto-Byzantine palace architecture helped determine the size, shape and appearance of the Villa/castello da Porto Colleoni at Thiene, the Dominante also created a villa type for its own purposes that was widely imitated too on the mainland in the later fifteenth and early sixteenth century. These lagoon villas, if they can be so described, were never intended to be at the center of large scale agricultural operations like a later generation of mainland villas. These were houses designed to stand in their own gardens, which were planted for the sake of ornament in the latest Renaissance fashion, but which also included plots of vegetables and herbs laid out in decorative patterns and which were connected by vine-draped pergolas to small orchards of fruit trees.

Of course, even for such a relatively limited amount of cultivation, these villas required much more land than the average palace in the city. Hence they were located far from the over-built center. Jacopo de'Barbari's aerial view of Venice dated 1500, a finely detailed woodcut, shows us some of these buildings and their gardens on the Giudecca. A few scattered examples of the villas survive today even farther afield at Mazzorbo in the northern lagoon, and the fourth order Gothic window frames on these suggests that they were built even earlier, around 1450. The great Gothic Palazzo da Mula on Murano is still clearly recognizable as a villa although even if it were not, there are many documented references to Murano's elaborate gardens, laid out with terraces, stonework, statuary and extraordinary fountains. The sixteenth-century Palazzo Trevisan on Murano is perhaps the most fascinating survival of this period and fashion. It was designed by Daniele Barbaro (1513–70), the learned patriarch of Aquileia who commissioned Alessandro Vittoria (1525–1608) and Paolo Veronese (1528–88) to decorate its rooms. This was the same team that worked for the Barbaro at Maser and more than one room in the house suggests that Palladio might have participated in the project. But it is the description of the vanished garden parterres that identify the palace on Murano as one of Venice's villas. These buildings were intended as suburban villas designed more for gardening and pleasure than for the more serious and extensive undertaking that agriculture represented on the mainland.

Venice's island villas were not very different from the palaces of the day, save that they stood isolated with regard to any other building. In terms of the subsequent evolution of mainland villas, the most interesting is certainly the one that appears in the foreground of Barbari's great woodcut map of the city. The most striking feature of this early sixteenth-century villa on the Giudecca is the ground floor arcade, designed with widely spaced columns supporting the fully semicircular arch so popular in Venice's early Renaissance period. This is a motif that appears often in mainland villas of the period and nowhere more beautifully than at the villa built by Queen Catherine Cornaro (1454–1510) for one of her ladies-in-waiting at Lughignano on the River Sile near Treviso. However graceful an architectural motif these arches may be, they were soon abandoned as the landowner's taste in architecture moved away from this tentative statement of Renaissance motifs to

a more assured, more archaeologically accurate revival of the vocabulary of classical antiquity in villa building.

But before discussing the full High Renaissance flowering of villa architecture in the sixteenth century under Jacopo Sansovino (1486–1570) of Venice, Michele Sanmicheli (1484–1559) of Verona and of Palladio himself, one other crucial element in the evolution of villa architecture in the Veneto must be mentioned. This is the farm outbuilding itself, which in the Veneto assumed a distinctive appearance and was given a distinctive name, the *barchessa*.

The typical Veneto *barchessa* is a long low building. The ground floor was used for stabling and for the storage of farm implements and tools while the upper floor, really an attic storey under the roof, became the granary. The *barchessa* must have assumed its definitive shape toward the end of the fifteenth century, because from that moment on it was always characterized by a long façade of arches of the type then popular. Of course this area provided extra space for the things that might be sheltered under it; it also effectively enlarged the granary above by extending the attic floor out over the front of the building. The *barchessa*, often attached to the block of the owner's house, also served as a decorative extension in the form of a long arcaded wing. Architects of every period respected the *barchessa's* function while exploiting its decorative possibilities, although they rarely modified the late fifteenth-century outline of its arcading.

The presence of a *barchessa* does not contradict the earlier generalization that the Veneto villa was a solid block of building like the palace in Venice. The *barchessa* was never a part of the house's living quarters but was essentially the barn, the granary, the stable and the farm outbuilding, even though attached to the house.

The villa of the Veneto was always principally and primarily a farm and not a country house or family seat. This point will be made again and again because it is essential to a correct understanding of both the purpose and the function of these buildings and their evolution in the history of architecture. Despite their purely functional purpose, the *barchessa's* decorative possibilities were always important to the villa's architect. In Palladio's great book on the principles of architecture, *I Quattro Libri dell'Architettura*, published in Venice in 1570, Palladio's woodcut shows the gigantic arcaded outbuildings of *barchesse* designed for the Villa Pisani at Bagnolo extending all around the farmyard, and enclosing an area the size of St. Mark's Square in Venice. The reference to that beautifully arcaded city square gives a hint of the respect he showed for the *barchessa* and its ornamental role in his building. Perhaps the most handsome of the *barchesse* designed by Palladio was that which survives – unlike those of Bagnolo which were destroyed by fire or those at Malcontenta which were never completed – at Fanzolo near Castelfranco. Eleven arcades extend on either side of the Villa Emo's classical, temple fronted central block – and eleven is a number which cannot be broken up into smaller units. The eye is unconsciously invited to scan the entire length of the *barchesse* from end to end, over and over again.

Palladio even extended this longitudinal sweep within the *barchesse* itself by cutting an open passageway through the ground floor of the house: the effect was that from one end of a *barchessa*, there is a view down the entire length of its arcade which continues

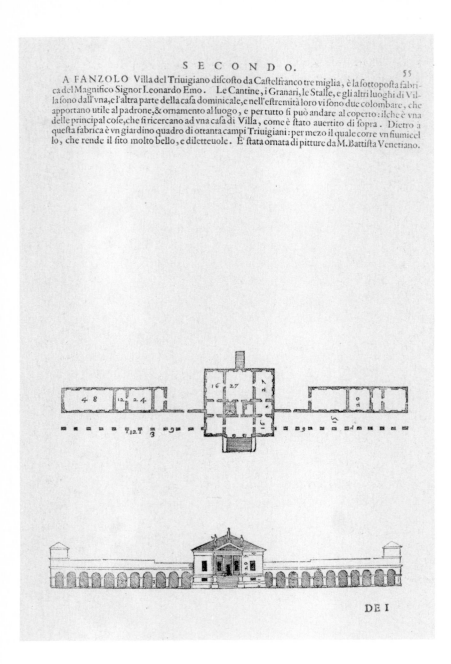

DE I

uninterrupted through the house to the long perspective of a diminishing arcade in the other wing. This long perspective axis through the *barchessa* was not an accidental device. Palladio used it again inside the Villa Barbaro at Maser where he transformed the *barchessa's* granary floor into an uninterrupted enfilade of living apartments running the entire length of both *barchesse*, at the end of which are splendid *trompe l'œil* frescoes by Veronese.

At both Maser and Fanzolo Palladio provided each *barchessa* with an architectural accent that created a sense of climax in these immensely long wings. On either end of the *barchessa* he erected dovecotes on the roof. At the Villa Emo these two constructions were quite unadorned, in keeping with the sober decoration of the building, whereas at Maser one is disguised with a large sundial and the other by the signs of the zodiac. The reasons for the differing ornamentation of these two will be discussed later, but for the moment it is sufficient to note that Palladio considered that the villa's dovecotes could be an integral part of the *barchessa's* two wings. This is because both of these houses were built by nobles from Venice, not by local landowners, and traditionally the Venetians kept in touch with the capital, the Dominante, through the use of homing pigeons. This emphasis on efficient communica-

tion with the capital also explains another feature typical of Veneto villas: they are usually built directly on a road or on a canal or other waterway that will lead to the city and its markets.

Building a villa in such a position may seem obvious to anyone familiar with the flat canal-crossed lands of the Veneto, where ancient Roman roads still cut a straight path across the landscape. However, the Veneto practice is quite at variance with villa building elsewhere during the Renaissance. For example, the Florentine architect and theorist Leon Battista Alberti (1402–72), basing his recommendations on the practice and writing of classical authors such as Pliny the Younger (AD 61–113), recommended that a villa be situated in such a way as to enjoy a view which encompassed the owner's own lands or some familiar landmark, panorama or prospect. A hilly eminence clearly suited his interpretation of classical antiquity best. His recommendations conveniently coincided with the fact that extant castles in Tuscany would have been built on hilltops and, as we have seen, could be used as the foundation on which to build a villa designed according to the latest, most fashionable Renaissance criteria.

The Veneto villa owner of the fifteenth and sixteenth century was just as interested in the ancients' exaltation of villa life as was his Florentine counterpart, but their approach and the approach of their architects was somewhat different. We are all familiar with Palladio's temple front portico applied to the façade of the Veneto farm villa. But even before the introduction of that novelty, probably first devised for the Pisani at Bagnolo, (although anticipated at Poggio a Caiano in Tuscany), the villa owners had borrowed yet another decorative device from the city in order to provide their villas with a suitably classical style ornamentation.

The Venetians had long enriched their palaces with coloured decoration, either in the application of semiprecious stone plaques and roundals or in the variegated marble columns which marked the *portego* window grounds on the *piano nobile*. There are references to the elaborate colouring used on the façade of the Ca' d'Oro on the Grand Canal early in the fifteenth century; and then in the early sixteenth century, the German merchants living and trading in their emporium at the foot of the Rialto bridge employed Titian (d. 1570) and Giorgione (1478–1510) to fresco the land and waterfront façades of their immense building with allegorical figures posed in the attitudes of classical statuary and framed in frescoed *trompe l'œil* niches. Fragments of this decoration have been preserved in one of Venice's museums, but there is virtually no trace of its widespread use on the façades of the city's palaces. Only faint shadows survive of Tintoretto's (1518–99) figures for the Palazzo Grimani, while traces of the more extensive cycles on the façade of Palazzo Loredan at Santo Stefano or Palazzo Martinengo at San Beneto have vanished forever. In the Veneto there is a great deal more evidence of the popularity of fresco decoration for the plain façades of the late fifteenth- and early sixteenth-century villas.

Frescoes of classical style medallions appear between fifteenth-century Gothic window frames on the façade of the Villa Monza-Mangilli at Dueville near Vicenza, while a house at Paese near Treviso is frescoed with patterns of an even earlier Gothic type. The frescoed decoration on the Villas Sernagiotto at Fossalunga di Vedelago, also near Treviso, includes a panoply of classical motifs led by the goddess Diana in the company of allegorical figures

Description, plan and front elevation of the Villa Emo at Fanzolo,
from Palladio's *I Quattro Libri dell'Architettura*, book II, ch.XIV, Venice, 1570.

representing Fame, Prudence and Rhetoric. The personification of Rhetoric serves to remind us of the degree to which the Renaissance, the rebirth of classical antiquity, was a literary movement. Latin authors such as Virgil, Cato, Varro and especially Pliny the Younger not only extolled agriculture as the noblest form of human activity, but also described the villa life of Imperial Roman times in loving detail. Eventually this literary inspiration transformed the villas of the Veneto into mirrors of classical Roman architecture in a way that neither the palaces of Venice, nor those of Florence, nor those of Rome ever surpassed. And while both Florence and Rome can claim a primacy over Venice and the Veneto in the revival of classical antiquity in Humanistic studies and in the application of classical motifs to the arts of painting and sculpture, none of the buildings of either of their provinces could compete with the extent to which the Venetians revived the vocabulary of classical antiquity in sixteenth-century villa architecture.

In the first part of the century, references to the architecture of classical antiquity were fairly tentative: either the arches of a loggia supported on the composite capitals invented in the previous generation by the Lombardo family of stonecutters, or else a plain stucco façade decorated in fresco with the gods and goddesses of pagan mythology. However, the sixteenth-century fresco work covering the entire façade of the Villa Corner-Piacentini near Castelfranco gives an indication of what was to come. Fluted Corinthian columns executed in *trompe l'œil* fresco rise to the roof through the two storeys of the villa's height. The plain round-arched windows of the central *portego* group are separated by a smaller set of correctly drawn columns and each window is crowned by a frescoed keystone made to look like a classical scroll bracket. After this, classical references no longer appear simply in fresco work imitation, but in beautifully modelled architecture and sculpture often executed by the finest artists available. Fresco work moves indoors and the repertory of life-size gods and goddesses keeps a brightly coloured company with the landowner and his family inside the house.

The most important source of classical antiquity for sixteenth-century Italy was, of course, Imperial Rome; by comparison Greek sculpture was still virtually unknown. In Rome itself, patrons and artists could still see many of the temples and buildings of the Forum standing intact. But it must be remembered too that, in the sixteenth century, Pompeii and Herculaneum had not been excavated so the architects of that century were completely dependent on the description of Pliny and others for their idea of the villas of Rome and the Empire. However, they did not have to travel to Rome itself – such travel was, in any case, arduous, expensive and rarely undertaken – for they could find fragments of Roman

Palladio's Villa Emo at Fanzolo, from O. Bertotti Scamozzi's
The Buildings and Designs of A. Palladio, vol. III, plate XIX, Vicenza, 1781.

19

buildings and ornaments scattered throughout towns like Padua, Vicenza or Verona. But no matter where they found their models, the architects and artists of sixteenth-century Italy were not interested in slavishly imitating the fragments they came across. They were more than willing to reinterpret the motifs of classical antiquity as best suited the taste of their patrons and, we may suppose, of themselves as well.

For example, the excavation of Nero's Domus Aurea in Rome led to the discovery of a room that was thought to have been the Emperor's grotto. Its decoration, consequently known as *grotteschi*, provided a popular theme in sixteenth-century art, although this was hardly ever executed in stucco relief, like the original, but rather reinterpreted in tempera or fresco paint. By the same token Palladio built some of his most impressive villa interiors by reinterpreting the ruins of the Baths of Diocletian. At the same time sixteenth-century architects often recognized the achievements of their contemporaries as worthy of the ancients. Michelangelo seems to have regarded Brunelleschi's dome for the cathedral in Florence (1420) in this way and Palladio himself published details of Bramante's Temple (1502) at San Pietro Montorio in Rome in the section devoted to antique monuments in his *I Quattro Libri dell'Architettura*.

The successful reinterpretation of motifs borrowed from classical antiquity could make the reputation of an architect working in sixteenth century Italy. For all the importance of Florence and the Medici family in fostering a radical reaction to over-elaborate Gothic taste in the fifteenth century, by the death of Lorenzo the Magnificent in 1492, the palm had passed to Rome where his son Giovanni and his nephew Giulio, as Popes Leo X (1513–21) and Clement VII (1523–34) respectively, would bring the great Renaissance papacy to a close. These two Medici popes and their predecessors made a contribution to Italian architecture that has often been overshadowed by the herculean task of continuing the reconstruction of St. Peter's Basilica. The popes were enthusiastic collectors of the fragments of antiquity that surrounded them in Rome and they were the first to seek to revive an aspect of Roman life that they had read about in the classics: the villas described by Pliny the Younger among others. However, since the popes had always to be resident in Rome, they ordered their architects to recreate the suburban villas of the great metropolis and not the great country houses in the midst of different estates. As they were understood by patron and protégé alike, these were villas close enough to the city for the pope to spend a pleasant day, to entertain his friends with elaborate banquets and then return to his city residence on the hills of the Vatican, the Quirinal or at the Lateran.

The suburban villas of classical antiquity suited the Renaissance popes to perfection and perfection is what Giulio de'Medici, later Clement VII, ordered from Raphael in 1516 and would have obtained at Villa Madama had his protégé lived longer. For all the villas built in or near Rome by the popes and their court of prelates and papal bankers, such as Agostino Chigi (1465–1520) at the Villa Farnesina, the great cardinals and bishops of the Renaissance church often required country houses farther afield. Pliny himself had lovingly described the number of villas he owned, scattered the entire length of the Italian peninsula, while in the sixteenth century, the immensely rich Cardinal Tolomeo Gallio, who had begun life as a fisherman's son, built so many villas that he could make the long journey from his northern diocese at Lake Como to Rome spending every night in a different villa of his own.

But before the princes of the church became quite so peripatetic, the suburban villa built on the outskirts of their diocesan town often satisfied their desire to have a pleasure pavilion near at hand, built in the very latest Roman fashion. This was certainly the case with the Bishop of Padua. Through the good offices of his learned administrator Alvise Cornaro, Bishop Francesco Pisani commissioned Giovan Maria Falconetto (1468–1534) to build him a pleasure villa at Luvigliano in the hills south of Padua. With its ancient Roman past, with its long tradition of classical learning and Renaissance Humanism fostered in its famous university, and with its contacts, through Giotto and then Donatello, with all that was most advanced in the arts of the Florentine Renaissance, the town of Padua proved the perfect agent for the introduction of the novelties of the Roman High Renaissance to the more conservative building traditions of the Venetian Republic. Falconetto had already built a classical Odeon for Alvise Cornaro who, in turn, would soon compose a treatise on the delights of villa life, *Dialogo della Vita Sobria*, full of Latin allusion and classical references and permeated by the high-minded seriousness which the ancients had bestowed on the cultivation of the earth and agriculture in general. Padua's role in the literary and intellectual revival of classical antiquity in Veneto villa architecture was still important in a later generation when Daniele Barbaro, rector of the university, edited and published for the first time since the Augustan era, Vitruvius's magisterial treatise on classical architecture. And later still, as a great prince of the church, Barbaro would become the patron of Andrea Palladio who had grown up in Padua.

In the meantime Falconetto received the commission to design a pleasure villa for the Bishop of Padua in 1529, two years after the sack of Rome by the troops of Charles V and the year before the last Medici pope would crown Charles Holy Roman Emperor in Bologna. Titian's presence in Bologna at this time could be said to mark a symbolic passage from Rome to Venice in the arts of Italy. The sixteenth century was undoubtedly Venice's golden age. Yet Falconetto's Villa dei Vescovi is the perfect illustration of the impetus given to this golden age from Rome, and not just from the Rome of classical antiquity, but from the Rome of the papacy as well. Despite the importance of Roman taste in modifying the appearance of villa architecture in the Veneto, it must be understood that this proved a relatively limited phenomenon in the long run – and the architects who built for Roman clergy in the Veneto soon found a far larger clientele among the local nobles and landowners who needed farm villas and not pleasure pavilions on their land.

In the meantime this fairly restricted category of suburban villas, built for the pleasure of rich prelates, did produce two of the most extraordinary buildings in the whole history of villa architecture: Falconetto's Villa dei Vescovi and Palladio's Rotonda; it also inspired a third, Scamozzi's Rocca Pisana, while helping to clarify the function of yet another, the Villa Barbaro at Maser. That the first three of these villas falls outside most of the conventions of Veneto villa building discussed so far is evident at a glance. Falconetto built his villa on a platform faced with fine rustication partly derived from Raphael's disciple Giulio Romano. Broad

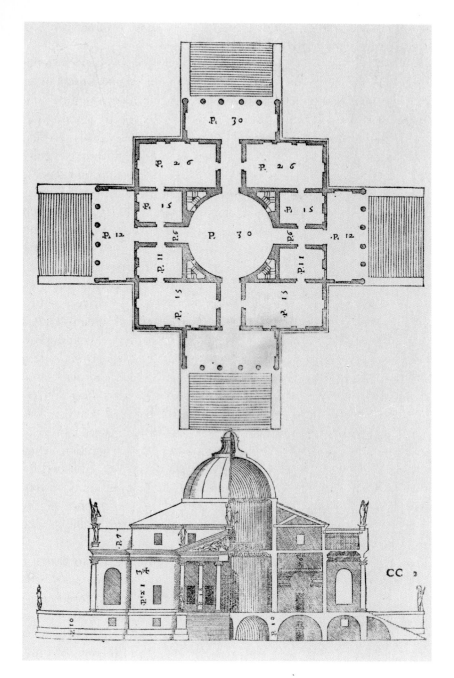

One of these rooms also contains a depiction of the several villas owned by the family in the eighteenth century. The symmetry of the interior plan was echoed in the four perfectly matched double arcades that surround the villas facing each point of the compass.

This correspondence between the external appearance and the interior symmetry of a villa was a novelty in Italian architecture; it did not exist in Falconetto's plan for the Villa dei Vescovi. It derived, not from Roman sources, but from the extreme symmetry of the Venetian palace floor plan where the *portego* provided the central axis on each floor for a series of identically shaped rooms on either side. However, it was Palladio who, with his sense of harmony and proportion, both internal and external, in both plan and elevation, must be given the credit for making this correspondence an integral part of villa building in the Veneto. The most striking example of his inventive powers along these lines lies in a villa that belongs to the same category as both Falconetto's Villa dei Vescovi and Varotari's Villa Capodilista. Whereas they were built as pleasure pavilions on the outskirts of Padua, one in 1529 and the other full fifty years later, Palladio's Rotonda was built on top of a hill outside Vicenza.

Like the Villa dei Vescovi, it was built for a powerful and wealthy prelate of the church, Paolo Almerico, who had returned to Vicenza after a long and successful career as a papal protonotary and apostolic referendary, high legal offices in the Vatican administration that earned him the rank of Canon of St. Peter's. He seems to have wanted a suburban villa in the best Roman fashion and he chose as his architect Palladio who was, by then, well known in Vicentine circles and who had visited Rome several times to study its monuments. Like Falconetto's masterpiece, the villa he built for Canon Almerico was situated on a hill and open to all points of the compass. The importance of the views it enjoyed put La Rotonda in a category far removed from the farm villas built in the Veneto before Palladio's day and different from those that Palladio himself was building within the limits of older conventions. The originality of the building is astonishing even today when photography has made us familiar with its progeny in every age and clime.

However much of its originality may be justly attributed to Palladio's genius, it is important to recall the sources of his inspiration. The name of the building provides the first clue. La Rotonda is also the popular name of the Pantheon in Rome, the great second-century Roman temple built under a vast dome open to the sky and preceded by an entrance porch of Corinthian columns. However, the original Pantheon temple rests on the ground whereas Palladio modelled the high base for his villa on other Roman temples, many of which were approached by a tall flight of steps. The domed center of Palladio's villa was obviously inspired by the Pantheon, and Palladio's dome was originally supposed to be open to the elements too. Directly beneath the central opening there is still a grotesque face carved in stone and set in the floor with holes through which the rain fell into a cistern located in the center of the ground floor next to the kitchens.

Despite the fact that the Rotonda was originally intended purely as a pleasure pavilion and Canon Almerico would never have spent the night in it, there were kitchens for the preparation of lavish banquets at which he entertained his friends. The owner would have avoided visiting the house on rainy days, not only because of

balustraded staircases rise to the single arcade that enclosed the house on three sides. Each arch is flanked by tall pilasters supporting a delicate frieze which approaches archaeological accuracy in the appearance, if not the proportions, of metopes alternating with triglyphs. The seven bays of each principal façade provide an anticipation of a motif – ultimately derived from Rome's Teatro Marcello – that Sansovino would use to great sculptural effect for his Libreria Marciana in the Piazzetta di San Marco some years later.

The idea of completely surrounding a hilltop villa with an arcaded façade was taken up again in the last quarter of the sixteenth century in a pleasure pavilion built by Dario Varotari (1534–96) for the immensely rich Capodilista family at Montecchia di Selvazzano. The villa is a two-storeyed building with four perfectly equal square rooms on the ground floor and four above. A narrow staircase rises from the front door to a landing where it meets a precisely equal ramp rising from the back door. Both stairways turn ninety degrees in opposite directions to reach the upper floor. Each room was frescoed in the style of Veronese by the architect whose principal fame derived from his talents as a painter.

Plan and front elevation of the Villa Almerico,
from Palladio's *I Quattro Libri dell'Architettura*, book II, f.19, Venice, 1570.

Marco Moro dis. e lit.   Lit. Ripamonti Carpi

the open dome, which was subsequently closed, but also because the great shutters closing the four doorways were removed, allowing those in the very center of the house to enjoy views in all four directions.

Students of the Rotonda usually concentrate their analysis on its remarkable external appearance and rarely bother to consider the way in which it functioned from inside, which was certainly the owner's primary concern. For example, a scholarly debate has grown up about the discrepancy between Palladio's woodcut illustration of the villa as published in the *Quattro Libri dell'- Architettura* and the actual finished appearance of the building. The illustration shows the villa with a drum rising through the attics to support a full blown dome, obviously inspired by Michelangelo's masterpiece for St. Peter's, whereas the villa today is crowned by a none-too-attractive covering reminiscent of a Chinese coolie's hat. Palladio's disciple is usually blamed for this solecism by scholars who have not found time to examine the interior of the building. Standing under the dome, it becomes perfectly obvious that it was completed as Palladio intended. It has those marvellous proportions that only Palladio knew how to bestow on a building. Indeed, if Palladio had added a drum inside the attic and put a dome on top of it, the effect from inside the building would have been akin to

standing inside a silo or a very tall cylinder with the decoration of the dome high above barely discernable.

The decoration of the dome may come as something of a surprise to the critic unversed in the taste of Palladio's patrons and times. The middle and late sixteenth century was the moment of highly developed Mannerism, not only in architecture but also in the decorative arts. The eighteenth-century Englishman may have copied Palladio's classical outlines, but his own taste in interior decoration was much more severe and even puritanical than that of Palladio's patrons. Men like Canon Almerico, bred to the classical culture of a Medici papal court, had no fear of extravagance or exuberance in their surroundings. The dome of the Rotonda is peopled with gods and goddesses, executed in fresco and in life-size plaster statuary. There are great ornamented cartouches and frames and the whole base of the dome is surrounded by a marble balustrade. On closer inspection, however, the balustrade is not marble at all, but wood painted to look like marble; similarly, the statuary is modelled in stucco to imitate stonework. These poor materials were not used for economy's sake because Canon Almerico and his like were certainly among the richest men of their generation. They were used because they could be modelled much more quickly than stone could be carved and also because the

Palladio's Villa Almerica Capra, with modifications to the cupola by V. Scamozzi, from Moro's *Vicenza and its Environs*, Vicenza, 1850.

weight of stone decoration would not have been safe in a brick and stucco structure such as a country villa. But there was another consideration that had more to do with decorum than with expediency or prudence.

The concept of decorum, much more familiar in the past than in our own day, sheds an interesting light on the decoration of villas in the Veneto in contrast to the decoration considered suitable for a palace or residence in the city. For example, whereas fresco decoration was sometimes used on plainer façades of sixteenth-century palaces in Venice, it made only a limited appearance inside the house. One room in a palace that was considered suitable for fresco decoration was the water entrance hall on the ground floor. Sadly most of this work, like that on the façades, has vanished from Venetian buildings, but documents speak tantalizingly of figures frescoed by Giorgione in the ground floor water gate of Palazzo Loredan at San Marcuola. For a palace's upper floors, the correct decoration would have been oil paintings hung on silk-covered walls in great gilded frames. Stamped and gilded leather was also a typical wall hanging in sixteenth-century Venice whereas tapestry played virtually no role whatever in Venetian interior decoration. The ceilings of a Venetian palace of this period were often covered with acres of oil paintings fitted into an elaborately carved and gilded framework, or else showed the building's wooden beams, picked out and embellished with more gilt decoration.

One of the differences between the decoration of city and country houses was the superabundance of gold and gilding in Venice and its complete absence in even the richest of country houses. Another indication of the distinctions that Venetians drew was in the use of stone ornament inside the house. The door frames in a city palace were usually made of marble even though such heavy material was otherwise generally absent in Venetian building. But stone made its most impressive appearance in the fireplaces in Venice's palaces.

The grandest palaces had fireplaces in the side rooms off the *portego*. The *portego* hall was only a gallery/corridor, never intended for use as a living room, but in the side rooms the lavishness of the fireplace knew no bounds: large fireplace hoods were supported by almost life-size caryatids carved in marble. They were frequently sculptured by the finest artists and in some cases, they were gilded as well.

The side rooms of the Rotonda offer an illustration of the different decoration deemed appropriate to a country house. As in the city palace, the villa's central hall had no fireplaces: the domed rotonda was as much a *portego* as was its rectangular counterpart in a more conventional farm villa. The walls of this central hall were covered with painted subjects, but they were executed in fresco, a much cheaper medium than oil painting – especially when the latter required gilded frames, or silk or gilded leather hangings as a backdrop. The decoration of the dome has already been described, while the ceilings of the side rooms were embellished with classical figures executed in fresco panels framed by heavy stuccowork borders. Again, this was far more economical, if not exactly rustic, when compared with elaborately carved and gilded wood framing for more oil paintings, typical of the city palace. The fireplaces at the Rotonda are very eleborate, but it is the hood that bears most of the ornament. Plain marble columns replace the city palace's caryatids while the hood was ornamented with stuccowork statuary executed

in high relief. All this stuccowork statuary in the dome and on the fireplaces suggests that there was another level of decorum: not only were distinctions made between the city palace and the country villa, but also between a suburban villa such as Canon Almerico's and a farm villa such as those that Palladio was building at the same time on more conventional lines for local landlords or for Venetian patricians. None of these farm villas had such highly ornamented fireplaces – often simply a plain stone frame almost flush with the wall would do – and even the richest did without marble details such as door frames. Even the lavish Villa Barbaro at Maser, built by the wealthy Patriarch of Aquileia, used *trompe l'œil* door and window frames painted in fresco.

The mention of fireplaces introduces another stage in the understanding of the Veneto villa and its functions. There is every indication that Canon Almerico resorted to the Rotonda in the summer months, escaping the heat of Vicenza and cooling himself in the breezes wafting through the high-domed hall. However, he and his successors there probably used the house in the spring and autumn as well. These were the seasons preferred by the farm villa owners and the fireplaces served to take the chill from the evening air in those seasons. Until the eighteenth century, the Venetians traditionally returned to the lagoon for the summer.

Frontispiece of Palladio's *I Quattro Libri dell'Architettura*, Venice, 1570.

Whatever uncertainty there may be about which season Canon Almerico intended to spend in the Rotonda, Palladio's disciple Vincenzo Scamozzi (1552–1616) produced a most wonderful hilltop villa, inspired by the Rotonda, which was definitely conceived as a summer house. La Rocca Pisana was not planned for a prince of the church, although it might well have been because it is certainly one of the most classical buildings ever built in sixteenth-century Italy, especially in its interior. As far as its exterior is concerned, it represents Scamozzi's slightly cold and academic reduction of Palladio's splendid, extravagant creation for Canon Almerico. La Rocca should be better known than it is, especially in the English-speaking world, as it was so clearly the model for Thomas Jefferson's famous, if slightly eccentric, creation at Monticello in Virginia. However, like many subjects of the great British Empire of his day and age, Jefferson preferred Palladio to Scamozzi, not that he would have been familiar with Scamozzi's work in the way that he was with Palladio's. His familiarity with Palladio was not based on first-hand experience since Jefferson never visited the Veneto or ever saw one of Palladio's dozen or so villas for himself. The reason for his preference lay entirely with Palladio's great book, *I Quattro Libri dell'Architettura*, which was published in 1570, shortly after the Rotonda was completed.

This book not only assured Palladio's high reputation and his widespread influence, especially in the world of the eighteenth-century British Empire, but also permitted Palladio's fame to eclipse that of every other architect working in the Veneto both before and after him. Like the earlier treatises of Vitruvius and Alberti, Palladio's book was a systematic exposition of the principles of architecture as it had been practised by the ancients and as it should be practised in the sixteenth century by all right-thinking gentlemen. He illustrated the book with plans and elevations of the ancient buildings he had studied and also with his own works: he even touched up his own buildings to make them appear more attractive in his illustrations. And this is the generally accepted explanation for the discrepancy that does exist between the dome of the Rotonda as it appears in the book and as it was completed in reality.

Scamozzi also wrote a book about architecture, *L'Idea dell'Architettura Universale*, which had the virtue of including medieval buildings as well as classical works; however, his approach to writing was perhaps overly theoretical and, like many of his churches and other buildings, a trifle too academic to reach the wide audience which Palladio enjoyed.

But some of Scamozzi's work was executed in collaboration with Palladio or at least completed what the Vicentine master had begun. The Rocca Pisana was built for the immensely wealthy Pisani family who had become feudal counts of Bagnolo under the Republic and who had commissioned Palladio to convert the remains of the Nogarola's castle into a great villa for them. The villa was intended as the center of a vast agricultural operation in the flatlands near Vicenza, but the feudal responsibilities which the Pisani acquired along with the Nogarola's estates probably kept them in the country much longer than was usual for the average Venetian landlord. This supposition is corroborated by the immense palace that they built in the neighbouring town of Lonigo and then by the fact that they hired Scamozzi to build La Rocca high on a hill not far away where they could escape the oppressively humid heat of the summer months in the plains.

The plan of La Rocca is based on that of La Rotonda, although the building's interior has been stripped of the Mannerist extravagances that characterized the decor of Palladio's masterpiece. Not only is Scamozzi's interior severe in the extreme, but the dome is still to this day open to the sky. This detail raises the question of furniture for such a villa.

It was not until the eighteenth century that the villas of the Veneto were furnished with their own permanent fittings. Sixteenth-century furnishings were meant to be transportable and would have arrived by ox-drawn wagons some time before the owner appeared to take up residence for longer or shorter periods. As we have seen, these visits may have been exceptionally brief in the case of the Bishops of Padua at Luvigliano, the Capodilistas at Montecchia or Canon Almerico at La Rotonda. But the objects with which they surrounded themselves, even if only for the day or for a festive occasion such as a country banquet, would have been just as magnificent as the houses they had erected for their occasional pleasure.

Great carved chests full to overflowing with rare velvets, silks and damasks would arrive at the house to be hung on walls or draped over the trestle tables of long planks set up for the entertainment itself. Other gilded oak chests contained Turkish carpets and delicate glassware from Murano or brightly coloured faience plates ornamented with classical motifs in imitation of the chasing and repoussé work of gold- and silversmiths. Heavy oak chairs and footstools would be assembled and set out with plump velvet-covered cushions. The owner's steward would take personal charge of silver and gold plate of the sort that survives today only in Veronese's representation of the Barbaro family treasure in a fresco panel decoration at Maser.

Of course, much of this splendour was in keeping with the great estate of a powerful and wealthy prelate accustomed to dispensing lavish hospitality.

The situation in the farm villa of the Veneto was quite different and subject to a different standard of decorum. But what is important to emphasize here is that for the sixteenth century and most of the seventeenth as well, the farm villa was only a seasonal residence for its owner. He sent his furnishings to the villa almost exclusively in the spring and the autumn, the seasons of sowing and harvest, and returned to the city in the summer to escape the heat in the cool stone vaulted rooms of his palace, or else to catch what breath of refreshment blew in with the breezes from the Venetian lagoon. The villa never became a country seat and the city palace remained the Venetians' principal residence.

The pleasure villas that have been considered thus far have provided an opportunity to discuss the ways in which certain elements of High Renaissance taste modified the villa building conventions of the sixteenth-century Veneto. This foreign, novel influence resulted in the creation of some of the Veneto's greatest masterpieces of villa design. However, these occasional pleasure pavilions or summer houses were not the norm for the landowners of the Veneto, nor for the Venetians who, thanks to the active encouragement of the Serenissima Repubblica, increasingly turned their backs on Venice's traditional seaborne commerce to invest their time and fortunes in reclamation and agriculture on the mainland.

The patricians of Venice who turned to agriculture in this generation were among the richest noblemen in Europe and they took to farming in the same grandly learned and intellectual terms that had inspired the Renaissance popes to build suburban pleasure villas near Rome on models suggested by classical authors. These Venetians were men whose parents had inherited the great Gothic palaces of the city or who had first built in the Florentine style as interpreted by Alberti's disciple Mauro Coducci (1440–1504), or else transmitted through the early Renaissance taste of the Lombardo family workshop of sculptors, stonecutters and architects. The Grimani family, one branch of which produced a veritable dynastic succession of Patriarchs of Aquileia for the church, employed Sanmicheli, the most Roman style architect they could find, to build an immense, classical-style palace for them near the Rialto. Sanmicheli came from Verona where he had designed palaces for a new street or *Corso* which extended between the Roman gate, *Porta Borsari*, to a triumphal arch built by Vitruvius when Verona was still a Roman city. Sanmicheli had borrowed motifs from both these structures and was clearly also inspired by Verona's great Roman arena. In the country he had designed a villa on the shores of Lake Garda, not far from Verona, for Count Agostino Brenzone, a Humanist author whose treatise on the pleasures of villa retreat, *La Vita Solitaria* (The Solitary Life) earned the praise of Pietro Aretino, the arbiter of Renaissance literary elegance.

Today, known as the Villa Guarienti, its regularly disposed, seven round-arched windows overlooking the lake recall the same number of arcades open to the view at the Villa dei Vescovi, although Sanmicheli's building is bare of architectural ornament. Originally, its plain façade would have been frescoed, but even without any classical ornament, its situation on the shores of the lake recalls the enthusiasm of Pliny the Younger for the views he enjoyed in his two villas overlooking Lake Como.

The lakes of northern Italy enjoyed great fame as the setting for splendid villas under the Roman Empire. The most extensive descriptions of these wonderful country houses appear in the letters of Pliny the Younger who was born at Como. Even earlier, the great poet Catullus (84–54 BC), who is claimed to have been born in Verona and who inherited a large estate in the neighbourhood, is known to have had a villa on Lake Garda, probably on the promontory of Sirmione. From time immemorial, the ruins there have been known as the Grotte di Catullo.

From these associations, it is clear that wealthy patrons of the Renaissance were drawn to the lakes as a setting for those villas which were to reflect their revived interest in the culture and customs of classical antiquity. However, this logical assumption is only partly true on two counts. First of all, there were not as many villas on the lakes in classical times as might be supposed. They were normally considered too far from the capital, the center of power in the Empire and therefore the only place for the ambitious to be. Villas so far afield were reserved either for the very rich or for retirement or for use in case of exile. That there were in fact villas on these lakes was only possible because of the *Pax Romana*, that extraordinary regime of peace, prosperity and security that extended over the whole of the Italian peninsula and even beyond its borders.

There was no *Pax Romana* during the Renaissance. In fact warfare had been an almost permanent condition of life in northern Italy since the Middle Ages, with city states and feudal territories in constant conflict.

One of the most famous of these endless battles actually took place on Lake Garda in 1438 when the Venetians sailed a fleet of twenty-five boats and six war galleys up the River Adige to its furthest navigable point and then dragged the entire fleet over fifteen miles of mountainous tracks to launch its warships on the lake. Two thousand oxen were employed, with one hundred and twenty pairs for each galley. From then on it was possible to speak of a *Pax Veneziana*, at least on Garda, although the great coalition, the League of Cambrai, soon disrupted the status quo in Venice's mainland Empire.

The first great villas were built on the lakes after the Peace of Bologna in 1530. In almost every case they were pleasure retreats for the great princes of the church – men who, like Cardinal Gallio of Como, may have been just as dependent on Rome as had been the servants of the Roman Empire, but whose secondary seat of power would be found in diocesan towns of the north. The fashions revived by these Renaissance prelates soon spread to that next most learned and literate class of sixteenth-century Italians, the classical scholar and Humanist. The Villa Guarienti was built overlooking Lake Garda for Count Agostino Brenzone. This villa was built on a promontory of the lake's eastern shore: the Punta di San Vigilio is approached by an avenue of gigantic cypresses which, in their magnificence, echo the grandeur of sixteenth-century villa life. It is still one of the most picturesque lake properties in northern Italy. The design of the immense block-like house is usually attributed to Sanmicheli who, with Sansovino, was the most important architect in the Venetian Empire before Palladio. The plain lake-front façade of the villa might have seemed oppressive in the severe simplicity of its architecture had Sanmicheli not opened it up to the view with the seven great windows spread across the garden terrace like a loggia, with an almost equally large range of windows on the upper floor. Such villas were intended as retreats for meditation and the serene contemplation of nature's beauty and God's creation. That these intellectual pursuits were enjoyed in the company of pagan antiquity is nowhere better illustrated than at San Vigilio, where a small garden terrace is surrounded by shrine-like aedicules, each containing the portrait bust of a Roman emperor.

In his own day, Sanmicheli may have been even more widely known than Palladio, since the Venetian state employed him to reinforce and reconstruct much of their military fortification at home and abroad. He surrounded Verona with a new circle of walls designed to withstand the heaviest bombardment; he built the Fortress of Sant'Andrea to guard the principal Lido entrance to the Venetian lagoon from the Adriatic and he devised the fortification of Crete which withstood twenty-one years of uninterrupted siege by the Turks over a century later. One of the country houses he built near Verona, the Villa della Torre at Fumane, is so overcharged with rusticated stonework as to seem more a fortress than a farm. This kind of ornamental dressing of stone – carving it so that it looked uncarved – was a Mannerist concept first used in northern Italy by Romano at Mantua, but ultimately deriving from the civic engineering of classical antiquity.

The most extensive ancient examples survive in the inner passageways of Verona's great first-century Roman arena.

Despite Sanmicheli's fame as an architect, his use of rusticated stone never became an important element of Veneto villa architecture. Stone was not available in most parts of the countryside, so brick and stucco remained the basic materials from which classical motifs were to be created. The first architect to incorporate the elements of classical antiquity into a farm villa was Sansovino. The building he designed for the Venetian Garzoni family was located not far from the Bishop of Padua's pleasure villa at Luvigliano. Villa Garzoni was built in about 1540, about ten years later than the Villa dei Vescovi and at just about the same time the younger Palladio was visiting Rome for the first time and using some of his new-found observations for the conversion of the Castello dei Nogarola into the Villa Pisani at Bagnolo.

What Palladio achieved at Bagnolo turned out to be ultimately more important and influential for the evolution of the Veneto farm villa, but Sansovino was also a great architect and his sole exercise in designing a country house deserves attention. One glance at the long white façade of the Villa Garzoni at Pontecasale shows that Sansovino intended to respect the villa building conventions that both he and Palladio, among all the others, had inherited from an earlier generation of farm houses in the Veneto. The building's great windows mark the importance of the *piano nobile*, and the way they are clustered in the center of the long façade makes the presence of a *portego* hall apparent. It will be recalled that all of this derives from a Venetian palace prototype and, in fact, the building closest in appearance to Villa Garzoni is the palace Sansovino designed for the Dolfin family at the Rialto. There too a long white façade – stone faced in the city just as it would be stuccoed in the country – is broken up with half columns, correctly ordered according to classical convention. A Florentine by birth, Sansovino was more than familiar with the classical vocabulary of the Renaissance; before coming to Venice in 1527 he had worked in Rome.

He designed many important buildings in Venice including the Libreria Marciana, which Palladio described as the "richest building since classical antiquity." Its long arcaded façade was charged with sculptured ornament, but the achitecture of the bays was borrowed, as Falconetto had done before him, from the Teatro Marcello in Rome. Both the Palazzo Dolfin and the infinitely grander Palazzo Corner della Ca'Grande on the Grand Canal had one-storey arcaded courtyards added to the back of the palace. Sansovino repeated this motif at Pontecasale, giving the Villa Garzoni a magnificently classical High Renaissance courtyard which is one of the great theatrical creations of country architecture in the Veneto. However, to his contempories, this courtyard might well have seemed excessively Roman and excessively urban in scale and magnificence, and just as the conservative Venetians did not develop a taste for palace courtyards in the city, no one bothered to copy Sansovino's wonderfully scenographic creation at Pontecasale.

Whether they were local noblemen or patricians from Venice, the villa owners in the Veneto seemed to prefer more practical solutions to such an outward show of wealth. For example, the Pisani at Bagnolo had accepted Palladio's transformation of their castle by vaulting over the former courtyard and opening up a three-arched loggia between the building's old towers. They also approved of rustication as a suitably classical embellishment for the façade of this loggia and were obviously pleased with the even more classical climax he provided in a great triangular pediment above this entrance. But the triangular pediment was not merely a decorative touch, and in fact it masks a large area for the storage of grain.

The villa Palladio built nearby for the Vicentine Pojana family was also provided with a similar granary under the roof of the villa. Here too Palladio masked the entrance to the main *portego* hall with a loggia, in this case decorated with a curious framing motif around the central arch that might have been borrowed from Bramante or possibly derived from the circular piercings Palladio introduced in the bays of the basilica in Vicenza. Whatever the source of his inspiration, it was not apparently a great success and indeed was never repeated in other villas of the Veneto. But for all the plainness of the Villa Pojana's exterior, its interior reflects aspects of Palladio's genius and the owner's taste that were common to many other farm villas built by the great architect. As in all Palladian villas, the plan is a masterpiece of symmetry with identically shaped rooms disposed on either side of the central hall; in elevation there is that sense of mathematical harmony that reveals the master's genius in a way that was never matched by any other architect. Perhaps all his followers or imitators sought to improve upon Palladio, but whenever they did, either in the Veneto or in eighteenth-century England, the first thing lost was Palladio's unique and inimitable sense of proportion. Subsequent patrons may have wanted more rooms or a larger hall or a more magnificent façade or a bigger house altogether, but without Palladio's genius, their architects never achieved more than a cold approximation of the grand, yet perfectly human scale of Palladio's originals. Palladio managed to imbue Pojana and every other house he ever built with this sense of proportion and the visitor is often surprised to find at Fanzolo or at La Malcontenta, that after approaching the house up a grand staircase and entering under an imposing classical portico, the back of the building lies less than fifty feet away from the front door. The relatively modest depth of these houses may have something to do with the fact that, although they sought to suggest the grandest classical ideals through their external architecture, the owner and the architect never lost sight of their purpose as country houses; their sense of decorum as well as economy recommended something suitable in scale to farming.

The grandeur of their classical conception of agriculture shows through vividly in the villas' interior decoration. The Pojana in their villa, or the Godi in the even plainer building Palladio designed for them at Lugo di Vicenza allowed classical allusion to run wild in great fresco cycles that often covered every wall with floor to ceiling extravaganzas of classical mythology, Rome's legendary history or a host of allegorical figures representing the Four Seasons or the Four Elements. As Roman and classical as these fresco cycles may be in their subject matter, they are undoubtedly the Veneto's most distinctive contribution to the art of painting. However, the finest of these painters are little known outside the Veneto because they painted only infrequently in oils, and their canvases are hardly ever to be found in museums. The two most famous, Giambattista Zelotti (1526–78) of Verona and Giovanni Antonio Fasolo (c. 1530–72) of Vicenza, were slightly younger than Palladio, but

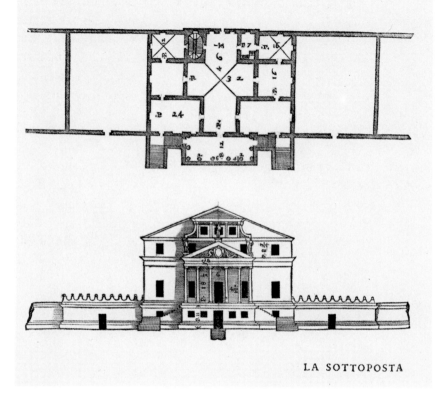

arms, the triangular pediment assumed a completely classical appearance as the crowning element of a portico that served no structural or architectural purposes in the villa at all.

The finest example of the temple front portico on a villa designed by Palladio is to be seen at the Villa Foscari at Malcontenta on the Brenta canal near Venice. The question arises as to why Palladio or the Foscari brothers who commissioned the building thought the temple front portico a suitable feature for a farm villa in the Veneto. The answer is a simple one. In the learned circles of sixteenth-century Italy, it was widely believed that the architecture of classical temples – that is to say, a colonnade supporting a pitched roof with gable ends covered by triangular pediments – ultimately derived from the domestic building types of the past. They thought that the Roman villa or even the Roman city palace inspired the architecture of the temples of classical antiquity. That this was an erroneous assumption was only proved two hundred years after Palladio's death with the excavation of the villas and palaces of Pompeii and Herculaneum.

In the meantime, this belief led Palladio and his patrons to add temple front porticos to the Veneto villa type in the hope that they were effectively recreating the country houses of ancient Rome. However, Palladio's approach to this goal was not quite as naive or as unsophisticated as it sounds when reduced to a simple formula. Palladio was willing to reinterpret – and his patrons expected him to – the canons of classical architecture. He did this in several ways with the temple portico: by recessing it flush with the block of the building at the Villa Badoer and the Villa Emo at Fanzolo, or reducing it to an element of sculpted surface ornament at the Villa Barbaro, or even treating it in a completely novel two-storey fashion at the villas built on the outskirts of Piombino Dese and Montagnana for the Cornaro and the Pisani families of Venice. These latter two reinterpretations are particularly interesting, not only because Palladio chose to represent the two-storey porticos as projecting on one side of the building and recessed on the other, but also because the double portico became one of the most widely copied elements of English Palladianism in the eighteenth-century southern states of colonial and ante-bellum America. Ironically enough, for all its popularity in the British colony of the eighteenth century, the double portico did not prove popular in the Veneto until after Palladio's death.

The temple portico motif is, more than any other single feature, the mark of Palladio in the Veneto villa. Yet inside these buildings there exists another element taken from classical models that was not merely a decorative feature and which Palladio himself probably believed essential to the spirit of these buildings as successful recreations of the villas of antiquity. This element is best seen in the elevation of such villas as the Villa Foscari, the Villa Malcontenta or the Villa Emo, but it is present in most of the others as well. In the three above-mentioned examples, the visitor enters a great central hall and proceeds around the compact block of the building, passing through rooms of diminishing height. The proportions of these rooms are so perfectly calculated and each is so impressive in its own scale, that it is only in the last of the series that the visitor becomes aware of how much the rooms have been diminishing in height as well as size.

The rooms of the Villa Emo at Fanzolo are among the very few

collaborated with him on more than one villa, and in his *Quattro Libri* Palladio usually identified the fresco artists with whom he worked. The finest of these cycles was painted for the Villa Barbaro at Maser by Veronese, whose artistic talent was so superior to all the other painters decorating Veneto villas as to make their work seem derivative from his.

These classical fresco cycles were not exclusive to Palladio's villas but, like Fasolo's cycle for the villa/castello at Thiene, appeared in even older houses as part of a scheme of interior redecoration. Indeed, very little of what has been described thus far concerning the villas of the Veneto was exclusive to Palladio. While his sense of proportion may have been unique, the famous symmetry of his floor plans derived from those of the Venetian palace. However, no discussion of the Veneto farm villa can be complete without reference to the one element of its architecture virtually invented by Palladio and used by him with such success as to become almost synonymous with Palladianism: the temple front portico. At the Villa Pisani it made a tentative appearance in the form of a large triangular pediment that disguised the presence of a granary under the steeply pitched roof. Later, this element becomes purely decorative, sometimes serving as the splendid frame for the family coats-of-arms as at Fanzolo or Maser. But even without a coat-of-

Description, plan and front elevation of the Villa Foscari, from
Palladio's *I Quattro Libri dell'Architettura*, book II, ch. XIV, Venice, 1570.

Veduta del Palazzo del N.H. Foscari alla Malcontenta.

actually built to dimensions that correspond exactly with the measurements that appear on the floor plan as published in the *Quattro Libri*. The great hall is 27×27 Venetian feet (a measurement virtually equal to the English foot) – in other words, a value of the mystical number three cubed $(3 \times 3 \times 3 = 27)$. The first lateral rooms on either side measure 27×16 – with the measure of three cubed now joined by one of four squared $(4 \times 4 = 16)$. The front room is actually a square room 16×16, while the link room measures 16×12 $(4 \times 4$ plus $3 \times 4)$.

In his brilliant study, *Architectural Principles in the Age of Humanism*, the art historian Rudolph Wittkower examined these relationships and concluded that Palladio and his patrons were dabbling in a numerology that suggested musical harmonies based on the mystical theories of Pythagoras. Ever since then scholars have debated whether this kind of mystical or harmonic numerology makes any difference to our aesthetic appreciation of a building or its interior. Of course such a debate can never be completely resolved since aesthetic experience is such a subjective category.

Palladio never included measurements of height on the plans he published, so the scholars who have debated the visual experience have often neglected to take this important component into account.

That it was an esssential element is obvious in a building like the Rotonda, although the domed hall is often seen as a unique tour de force and seldom in relation to the progression of its side rooms, which diminish in height. The best clue to the source of Palladio's interiors is to be found in the Villa Foscari at Malcontenta where the central hall is lit by a bank of windows crowned by a great semicircular lunette divided into sections by two upright elements. Palladio took this window design from the Roman ruins that obviously impressed him most of all and which he studied in their every detail: the great Baths of Diocletian, part of which Michelangelo converted into a Christian church in 1563. The Villa Foscari's lunette window derives from these ruins and its type is still called a "thermal window" by art historians. But the aspect of the Roman Baths which impressed Palladio most, and which he subsequently reinterpreted in many of his villa interiors, was the progression through the building in rooms of diminishing size, and even more importantly, diminishing height. The Roman of antiquity would leave the great, immensely tall *frigidarium* for the lower, smaller *tepidarium* and finally reach the *caldarium*, the smallest and lowest chamber in the vast edifice. That this progression was a practical consideration essential to the nature of the Baths did not

Palladio's Villa Foscari "La Malcontenta," from G. Costa's, *Villas of the Brenta*,
plate XIII, Venice, 1711–72.

28

bother Palladio at all. He, like most of his contemporaries, was willing to reinterpret the elements of classical architecture to suit himself and his patrons. From the evidence available at Pompeii and Herculaneum, this progression in size and height was never part of villa construction or design in classical antiquity.

To return briefly to the aesthetic debate mentioned earlier, Palladio's rooms were conceived not only in terms of the measurements printed on his floor plans, but also in terms of their height. Inside the rooms this is most evident in the size, shape and especially in the position of the doors and the windows. The latter are usually perfectly proportioned in relation to the room and the wall in which they are set; however, their position may also take into account the situation of the fireplace, thereby frequently producing a strange, unbalanced or even asymmetrical result on the building's exterior which architectural historians are at a loss to explain away. But for all the building's external appearance and magnificence there is here every indication that Palladio designed the interior as the most important component of the building and, of course, in doing so he would most please his patron who had to live in it.

It is the interior of the Villa Barbaro at Maser that explains many of the contradictions implicit in this richest and probably most famous of all Palladio's creations. From the outside, the house seems to belong to the category of a Veneto farm villa. There are the long *barchessa* wings crowned at either end by dovecotes. The central section of the villa is quite obviously the residential block with a great family coat-of-arms carved in the triangular pediment of its temple front façade. But then the contradictions begin to appear: the temple front is not rendered as a portico, but as a decorative motif sculpted in high relief and it is divided into two floors instead of masking a single elevation. The villa also appears situated on an unusually high eminence in comparison with other farm villas, although Palladio designed the building so cleverly as to mask completely the slope of the hill on which it stands. It is only inside the building that these discrepancies begin to resolve themselves, but only in surprising, if discreetly veiled terms.

First of all, a staircase under the *barchessa* wing hidden at the side of the main block rises to the *piano nobile*. The alert visitor realizes that the central hall in which he stands is only one storey high – unlike that at the Rotonda, the Villas Emo or Foscari or any of the others – and is located virtually under the roof. Yet at the back of the house a door opens directly out into a garden at ground level. When approaching this level at the back of the house the visitor encounters on either side an enfilade of rooms built through the upper floor of both *barchessa* wings where, in a normal farm villa, the granary should be. This single anomaly reveals that Palladio's patrons did not intend him to create a simple, straightforward working farm villa for them. While it was the hillside site that determined the location of the principal apartments on the upper floor of the main block, thus also giving access to the granary level of the *barchessa*, the Barbaro obviously chose this particular site with the recommendations of classical antiquity in mind – especially when Latin authors such as Pliny had praised the views to be enjoyed from a height.

Palladio's principal patron Daniele Barbaro represented both aspects of the cultural connection between the Veneto and Rome that have been discussed earlier. He was the editor of Vitruvius's treatise on classical architecture and he was a prelate of the Roman church. Indeed he was the Patriarch-elect of Aquileia when he and his brother, Marc'Antonio, employed Palladio to build the villa at Maser. The Patriarchate, a unique sinecure that was later abolished, made its incumbants the richest prelates in western Christendom after the Pope. The wealth, learning and the artistic ambitions of the Barbaro brothers reveals itself in many aspects of the building's function and appearance, and nowhere more so than in the small enclosed garden at the back of the house. It seems that the owners themselves designed the Nymphaeum that acts as a backdrop to the garden. A statue of Diana crowns the composition. The water from a spring in the hillside spurts from her breasts into a fishpond built into the pavement at the villa's back door. There is a grotto beneath the statue of the goddess where a reclining river god also pours spring water into this small pool. But none of this was intended to be purely decorative. The allegorical statues standing around the edge of the pond are part of a learned programme whose precise meaning has eluded even the most scholarly students of the villa today. But beyond this, the water from the pond was channelled by Palladio into two conduits, one which led to the kitchens to provide running water there, and the other which went to the stables and was again divided on the one hand into the drinking troughs and on the other along a gutter to facilitate the cleaning and mucking out. All this water then flowed down the slope in underground channels to irrigate the garden parterres and reached the bottom of the hill with enough force to activate a great fountain crowned by a statue of Neptune, designed by Vittoria.

The fountain stood on the road and functioned as a drinking trough for passing horses; the water then went on to irrigate the orchards and fields laid out in the distance. The whole system was in fact a triumphant homage on the part of the Barbaro brothers to the hydraulic engineering of Roman antiquity. Of course, this subtle programme is not the most famous aspect of the villa, nor are the even more recondite frescoes, probably based on the Barbaro horoscope, as widely understood as they might have been in the sixteenth century. However, even though the programme of this decoration remains obscure, its fame as an absolute masterpiece of sixteenth-century fresco painting is universal. They were painted for the Barbaro brothers by Veronese. Some of the villa's rooms are frescoed with allegorical figures suggesting classical virtues or gods and goddesses, but there are others which seem more like lighthearted jokes or which represent landscapes framed in elaborately conceived *trompe l'œil* architecture. These views of the countryside are in fact the very first pure landscape painting in the history of European art.

The fresco decoration of other Veneto villas may not enjoy such great fame or even have such an important position in the history of European painting, but many of them suit their context to perfection. Such is the case at Fanzolo where the series of frescoes on classical themes by Zelotti is one of the finest in existence. Apart from illustrating archaic Roman legends and virtues, there are scenes which refer directly to the cultivation of the Emo's land at Fanzolo. The pure functionalism of the Villa Emo as a working farm seems to be reflected in the sobriety of its architecture, especially compared with the richer details of the Villa Barbaro at Maser. And this contrast does correspond to reality since Leonardo

Emo was neither a prince of the church nor an academic, but a Venetian patrician who enthusiastically and intelligently complied with the Republic's policy of land reclamation for the benefit of agriculture. He introduced the cultivation of maize into Veneto agriculture, thus replacing the peasants' millet with a more nourishing foodstuff that remains an essential part of the diet of northeastern Italy to this day. His direct descendant still farms the land at Fanzolo four hundred years later, but no longer resides in Palladio's splendidly proportioned central block. Like every other sixteenth-century farm villa in the Veneto, the main house at Fanzolo was meant to be inhabited – and this cannot be emphasized too often – only during the season of the sowing and the season of the harvest. For the rest of the year, including the hot summer months, the Venetian patrician or the local landowner retreated to his house or palace in the city.

The beautiful long *barchessa* wings of the Villa Emo were converted into a series of living apartments in the eighteenth century. This was highly unusual and probably reflects more the taste of a specific generation of the family than a general tendency. Even earlier the Emos at Fanzolo had converted the right-hand *barchessa* into a heated breeding nursery for the raising of silkworms, but this did not prove to be the success they anticipated. In any case there can be no question that the patterns of agriculture were shifting, as was the incidence of great wealth invested by Venetians in the mainland. The local nobles of Vicenza, Verona and Padua had suffered particularly as a result of crop failures and the subsequent collapse of the banks in their native towns.

More of Palladio's magnificent palace designs could be completed in Vicenza and many of his plans for villas remained unrealized, yet there were still families who continued to build villas in the Palladian style at the end of the sixteenth and well into the seventeenth century. The Villa Emo at Rivella is a particularly handsome example of the persistent popularity of Palladio's temple front portico motif on a Veneto farm villa. Eventually the entire repertory of Palladian themes was revived in the eighteenth century when Venice and the Veneto enjoyed a second golden age in the arts and in architecture. The persistence of the Palladian style in country house architecture led to many villas being described in the captions of eighteenth-century engravings as "by Andrea Palladio" when such an attribution was beyond the limits of chronological possibility.

Palladio's own disciple and sometime collaborator, Scamozzi, was partly responsible for the continued importance of the Palladian prototype, as we have seen at La Rocca Pisana. He also built a villa for the Molin family which was even closer in appearance to its Palladian prototype, the Villa Foscari at Malcontenta. But Scamozzi had no more success than any other imitator in capturing the essence of the Palladian interior: harmony and proportion. In addition, most of Scamozzi's villas were too academic and cold for the taste of the seventeenth-century noblemen. They chose the Maser version probably because it was, ironically enough, the more economical both in terms of cost and in terms of space consumed. It represented temple columns in bas-relief, half columns as it were, that did not take up any of the building's interior space, as in the cases where Palladio had recessed the portico flush with the façade, nor did it cost as much to build as a projecting porch which, in any

case, had no real practical or structural function. The Maser-type temple front façade was not only used on Veneto villas built throughout the seventeenth century, but also appears on two of the grandest examples of eighteenth-century villa architecture as well – the Villa Marcello at Levada and the Villa Pisani, now known as the Villa Nazionale at Stra on the Brenta.

But in the intervening period between Palladio's death and Venice's second golden age in the eighteenth century, Veneto villa architecture definitely played a secondary role in the European scale of things. Palladianism might well have become an important cultural force in England had not its principal patron Charles I, King of England, been overthrown and executed in 1643. In fact, seventeenth-century domestic architecture in Europe usually owed more to Holland and to the rich and powerful Dutch Republic than it did even to Baroque Rome. Venice continued to construct buildings both in the city and on the mainland during these hundred or so years, but her greatest native architect, Baldassare Longhena (1598–1682) is better remembered for his pilgrimage church of Santa Maria della Salute or his palaces for the Pesaro and Rezzonico families in Venice than he is for his possible intervention at the Villa Tiepolo at Carbonera near Vicenza. The seventeenth century in the Veneto represented either a continuation of Palladian motifs or a stylistic eclecticism or else an attempt to impress by sheer size.

The handsome sixteenth-century Villa Allegri at Cuzzano di Grezzana owes its present appearance to architectural and decorative elements added in eclectic fashion during the seventeenth century, while the Villa Contarini at Piazzale del Brenta became, in that same period, the largest villa in the Veneto by virtue of the extraordinary long and impossibly grand wings that were simply added on to the relatively modest and quite conventional central block of the building.

For all this discussion of sophisticated architecture and ornament, whether it be in the purest Palladian style or in a more decadent taste, the average Veneto villa was more often a suitably simple and conservative building. It still owed a great deal to the older conventions of villa architecture as they derived from Venice's palaces. It was a solid brick block, two, occasionally three storeys high, with a plain façade covered with stuccowork and ornamented only by the bank of windows in its center providing illumination for the long *portego* hall on the *piano nobile*. But these same plain buildings did come to reflect something of the exuberance of Baroque taste, especially as the Republic's second golden age – the age of Tiepolo, Goldoni, Vivaldi and Canaletto – began to dawn. Gesticulating stone statuary, often carved by Orazio Marinali (1643–1720) or members of the prolific Muttoni dynasty of stonecutters and sculptors, would be added to the peak and points of a simple triangular pediment to give the building a somewhat makeshift air of classical grandeur. Palladio had often foreseen such accents in statuary for his own villas in an earlier generation, but the sixteenth century was not attuned to the kind of workshop organization that made it possible to turn out a sufficient quantity of these pieces in stone for the purposes of decoration.

Besides joining the capped chimneys and the obelisks that were the characteristic ornament of villa rooflines in the Veneto, stone statuary found an even more congenial setting in the gardens of the villas. Marinali's statues were often carved in the lively attitudes of the characters of the *Commedia dell'Arte*, the improvised comedies, originally performed by itinerant players from Bergamo and based on a few local characters, that were particularly popular in the lands of the Venetian Republic in the seventeenth and eighteenth centuries. Many villa gardens were not only populated by these figures in statuary, but also had theaters made of box hedge for actual performances by the itinerant companies. Stone provided other accents for the formal garden in the Veneto besides statuary. There were benches, steps and beautifully carved balustrades as well as elaborate fountains and gateways. The gardens of the Villa Barbarigo at Valsanzibio are an excellent illustration of the degree to which ornament was lavishly used in gardens of this period. All this may come as something of a surprise to the visitor since the villa itself is so plain and unassuming. The surprise would have been even greater in the eighteenth century when the property could still be approached from Venice by boat. The visitor disembarked in front of an enormous ornamental gateway and climbed past an elaborate series of fountains to turn at right angles along a long boxwood-hedged avenue. Behind each wall of tall hedge the garden had secret rooms, created in boxwood, to contain allegorical statues with esoteric astrological significance; a labyrinth whose tortured path may have been part of an overall programme of initiation into arcane mysteries; and a moat-surrounded island where rabbits cavorted to the delight of the guests. The owner would be amused when secret jets of water doused his unsuspecting visitors as they sat down on the stone garden benches to take their rest from the long walk up the avenue to the villa.

As characteristic as all this may have been of the eighteenth century's obsession with amusement, life in the Veneto villa was sometimes cast in the grandest possible setting. Such was the case in the Villa Marcello at Levada where the central hall or *portego* rose through a full two storeys of the house. Here the central hall seems more like a ballroom than like the *portego* of earlier traditions. The Marcellos and others of their generation commissioned the finest fresco artists from the city to decorate the walls and often the ceilings of their villas. The subjects were still the legends and deities of classical antiquity, but these vast compositions were now surrounded by a frivolous framework of rococo stucco. Nowhere in the Veneto are the delights of this particularly Venetian art more evident than at Levada. The upper bedrooms contain stucco panels worked with a naive charm that marks the style of an itinerant "stuccador" rather than a sophisticated artist from the workshops of the city.

The villa's furnishing would also reflect eighteenth-century taste as much as did the frescoes or stucco decoration. Furniture was now made on the estate and left in the house. It copied the rich and fashionable curves of Venetian pieces, although in the country the plain wood was allowed to show through. One of the most typical pieces was reserved for the main hall or *portego*. This was a long settee, often extending over five or seven places, with a cane or straw seat and a back carved in sinuous curves or ribbon motifs popular in the first half of the eighteenth century. This formal piece still served to indicate that the *portego* or main hall of the villa was not really a living room, but a passage, a corridor, or even the ballroom of the building. Hardly any of the furniture made for the villas — called *mobili di villeggiatura* — was gilded or lacquered, as it would have been in the city, although a few distinctively Venetian lacquer pieces may have been intended for the country, as their name *lacca povera* implies. This was a kind of "do it yourself" technique that was considered, in town and country alike, suitable employment for the ladies of the house. The piece of furniture chosen for this kind of decoration was usually the tall bureau bookcase of the type called a *trumeau* in the Frenchified Venetian fashion of the day. A trumeau or a chest of drawers gave the amateur lacquer artist more surface on which to work than did seat furniture or a settee. Basically the piece was painted the pale colours of the professional cabinetmaker's palette and then engraved subjects cut from a book of designs would be applied and coloured (or not) to suit the owner's taste. The piece was then varnished over with a shellac whose gloss imitated real lacquerware while the engraved outlines of each scene showed through like the brush strokes of the professional artist.

The Villa Marcello is to this day a working farm and it is important to remember that, even in the age most notorious for frivolity, the majority of the villas in the Veneto were devoted to serious agriculture. This is corroborated on the grandest possible scale at the Villa Manin at Passariano, the villa of the last Doge of the Republic. The villa itself was plain enough in the conventional way although the Manin's legendary wealth (one of the reasons he was elected Doge despite not being a native Venetian) is reflected in the wonderful frescoes by Gian Battista Tiepolo (1696–1771) which decorate the main hall of the house. However, the villa's most impressive feature is the arcaded precinct in front of the building where the *barchessa's* arcades are continued across the road to enclose a vast area on the other side. The road brought all the neighbouring peasants and villagers to the space in front of the villa for their weekly markets and with this splendid and spectacular piece of architecture the Manin gave shelter and protection to these gatherings. The scale and extent of this precinct recalls the area Palladio planned to enclose two hundred years earlier at Bagnolo for the Pisani family, but while Palladio's design was meant to echo the arcaded enclosure of Venice's St. Mark's Square, the Manin's architect clearly sought to suggest an even more currently fashionable square — none other than Bernini's colonnaded forecourt in Rome for St. Peter's.

Although both the Villa Marcello and the Villa Manin could be taken as a suitable conclusion to this summary introduction to the world of the Veneto villas, their function as farm villas leaves little or no room for the most famous aspect of Veneto villa life in the eighteenth century. It was during this last century of the Republic's existence that villas began to be built in the Veneto merely for pleasure. In a way, this was a return to the pleasure pavilions built in the early sixteenth century by those powerful princes of the church who sought a fashionable retreat from the cares of the world in an isolated suburban villa not far from their home town or their diocesan seat. We have looked briefly at those villas and their progeny in the Euganean Hills near Padua, or near Vicenza's Monte Berico and even on the shores of Lake Garda, but now, in the eighteenth century, we return again to the *Dominante*, to Venice herself, and to an entire suburb of villas built almost entirely for pleasure and for summer holidays on the banks of the famous Brenta canal.

Literally hundreds of villas line the Brenta from Padua to the point where the canal joins the Venetian lagoon at Fusina. Some of them, like the Villa Foscari at Malcontenta, had been there since Palladio's day or even earlier, when the Republic encouraged the reclamation of this territory for cultivation. Most of the families who built villas on the Brenta were from Venice, given its proximity to the lagoon. Several of them built more than one house there, especially in the eighteenth century when Venice was struck by what Goldoni satirized as *smania di villeggiatura*, the mania for villa holidays. More than one of these houses is exceptionally long, for example La Barbariga or the Villa Contarini at Piazzola, with *barchesse* which now served as sheer decoration with barely a hint of their former function and purpose. While many of the Brenta villas reflect a continuing conservatism in architecture and a fidelity to older conventions, the one area of extravagance in which they most often indulged was the conspicuous consumption of space. No better example of this exists on the shores of the Brenta today than the gigantic Villa Pisani at Stra.

The Pisani family was one of the most prominent in eighteenth-century Venice. It had long proliferated in many branches, with the richest, known as the Pisani del Banco, resident in the parish of San Vidal. Like all great banking families of every era, they seemed able to gather all unto themselves and later in the eighteenth century they even absorbed the wealthy Pisani-Moretta branch of the family who held the county of Bagnolo in awe with its massive villa designed by Palladio and its summer pavilion, La Rocca, designed by Scamozzi. At the beginning of the eighteenth century, however, the Pisani del Banco's proudest possession was undoubtedly their massive palace at San Vidal which had been under construction since the preceding century. It was an immense affair that already incorporated two huge theatrical courtyards, an unheard-of extravagance in a city where building space had always been at a premium. Indeed the Venetian government found this consumption of space far too conspicuous and forbade its continuation and completion. Had the building been allowed to proceed, the palace would have reached the Grand Canal, completely engulfing the two palaces that stand there now, while behind the new canal frontage, the Pisani palace would have found room for yet a third gigantic courtyard. But the Pisani del Banco were not to be baulked of their glory, even if it could not be realized in their own parish of San Vidal.

In 1735 a distinguished member of the family was elected to the highest office in the millennial Republic as Doge Alvise Pisani. The Pisani decided to celebrate the event with a monument which would ever more resound to the glory of the family. They commissioned a huge villa on the banks of the Brenta at Stra, not far from another Villa Pisani known as La Barbariga. The architects of this great masterpiece of eighteenth-century extravagance were Girolamo Frigimelica (1653–1732), who had already designed many of the ornamental gates and outbuildings in the park and had long worked on the palace at San Vidal, but who died before the villa got under way, and a neo-Palladian architect from Castelfranco Veneto, Francesco Maria Preti (1701–74). In the end the villa was Preti's triumphant invention, just as the tiny opera house he designed for his home town represents the delightful charm of much eighteenth-century Veneto culture. But what Preti created at Stra was really more suited to the grandeur of a sovereign prince than to commemorate the election of a banker to high political office.

The Villa Pisani at Stra is a building that contrives to be beautiful at the same time its size and scale seek to overwhelm. In this it makes use of a Palladian sense of proportion within a scale that Palladio would probably have found unacceptable. Nonetheless all the Palladian components are there, even if a little more abundantly than Palladio might have thought suitable to a country house. Preti even embellishes the simple rusticated base of his immensely long canal-side façade with giant caryatids – a motif more suited to eighteenth-century Vienna than to a country road in the Veneto. The two inset wings of the building are twin Palladian palaces taken from the streets of Vicenza, while the temple front portico in the center more than doubles its original at Maser.

But such a cursory description of the façade does no justice whatever to the scale of the building. This cannot be appreciated by anyone who has not walked through the two huge courtyards incorporated into the fabric. The garden beyond reveals the vast extent of the Pisani's undertaking at Stra. An enormously long pond, a *tapis d'eau* worthy of Versailles, stretches the length of the central axis and is only closed by a palace rising at the end of the garden. This second building is an even finer exercise in Palladianism than the villa itself because here the architect could concentrate his talents on creating a façade with no thought to the building behind. The visitor might be forgiven for thinking he had come upon a magnificent compendium of every sixteenth-century architectural concept, perfectly preserved in the midst of an eighteenth-century park. But such a visitor's astonishment would only be compounded if he knew what lay behind this wonder. For this tour de force of High Renaissance architecture was created simply to mask the Pisani's stables. This stable block and all the ornaments of the park were Frigimelica's work before the villa was begun. The house itself rises to great heights, too, although not at the hands of the architect. The Pisani chose the greatest exponent of Venice's second golden age to depict the glory of their house and name. The *Apotheosis of the House of Pisani* was painted over the vast ballroom by Tiepolo just before he left Italy forever to work for the King of Spain. Tiepolo's vision of the Pisani's glory opens directly into the heavens, but as in all of his work, the actors in this great celestial *tableau vivant* are dressed in the costume not of his own eighteenth century but in the doublets and hose, the capes and décolletage of that first great golden age of Venice and of her villas in the Veneto, the sixteenth century. Tiepolo's homage to the Pisani is thus clothed in the era he most admired: the age of Veronese and the age of Palladio – one of the brightest, most soaring moments in the history of European culture and civilization.

Peter Lauritzen

Villa Foscari "La Malcontenta," Malcontenta, Venice
The architecturally captivating north-facing side of the villa, which was intended as the formal
entrance. The austere dignity of the temple front portico and pediment, and the high socle of the
Ionic loggia, reflected in the river below, make this the noblest realization of the Roman dream. The
steps on either side seem timidly to acknowledge the formal grandeur of the villa.

Villa Foscari "La Malcontenta," Malcontenta, Venice
In this Stanza dei Giganti (Room of the Giants), which Battista Franco left unfinished on his death
in 1561, the artist reveals his careful study of Michelangelo and his admiration for the similar room
in the Palazzo del Te in Mantua, frescoed by Giulio Romano thirty years earlier. The dramatic
impact is increased by the powerful interplay of light and shade, in contrast with the serenity of the
sky and the frailty of the tree, while Jupiter looms menacingly overhead.

Villa Foscari "La Malcontenta," Malcontenta, Venice
Cryptically allusive grotesques by Giambattista Zelotti decorate the small rooms arranged
symmetrically on either side of the main hall. Palladio's design called for large, medium and small
rooms to be adjacent to each other, such as a *studiolo*, a library, or a room in which to store riding
gear and other everyday items.

35

Villa Foscari "La Malcontenta," Malcontenta, Venice
There is perfect spatial balance and decorative harmony in the central hall with its frescoes by
Giambattista Zelotti. In the center of the ceiling, a hexagon depicting the Virtues links the four vault
ovates in which Astraea is portrayed presenting Jupiter with worldly pleasures; two women offer
Janus incense; Jupiter bestrides an eagle with Mercury, and Midas sits on his throne with Envy
while Discord confronts them. Festoons and cherubs adorn the spaces in between.

Villa Foscari "La Malcontenta," Malcontenta, Venice
Painted wooden sculptures of Ariosto's characters, Rinaldo and Armida, on the ground floor of the
villa, Rinaldo is shown less as as a warrior than in a pose suggesting a declaration of love.

Villa Foscari "La Malcontenta," Malcontenta, Venice
Fresco of the "Malcontenta," the discontented woman. According to the historian Pompeo
Molmenti, tradition has it that this villa took its name from a beautiful girl from the Foscari family
who was sent to live there by her parents for the sins she had committed. In fact, the name seems to
derive from the discontent of those living there after the Paduans ordered the surrounding farmland
to be flooded, causing the abbey of Sant'Ilario to become an island.

Villa Foscari "La Malcontenta," Malcontenta, Venice
The impressive main hall: the elegant south-facing window lets in a flood of bright light which sets
off a continuous display of visual echoes, heightening the magical tone of Zelotti's frescoes and the
purity of relationship between the vaults.

Villa Foscari "La Malcontenta," Malcontenta, Venice
The southern façade of the villa, overlooking the open country. Here Palladio has created a different kind of
impact to reflect an essentially rustic character. The middle section of the façade barely stands out from the rest,
while the triangular tympanum is set into the wall as a purely ornamental feature, with a gap in its base-line to
accommodate the top of the thermal window. This, together with the three windows beneath, makes up a group
of six openings through which light streams into the great main central hall.

41

Villa Pisani "La Nazionale," Stra, Venice
Of all the villas, "La Nazionale" on the banks of the River Brenta at Stra, once the seat of the Pisani
family, is certainly the largest and most elaborate. It most faithfully conveys the sense of the
luxurious life style led by noble Venetian families at a time when rivalry in wealth was the leading
form of ostentation – eventually leading to the decadence and decline of the Venetian Republic.

Villa Pisani "La Nazionale," Stra, Venice
This column-lined atrium, between two elegant courtyards, saw the arrival and departure of guests
at receptions both large and small. Visitors were welcomed in exotic reception rooms, decorated in
Turkish, Chinese or Persian style. There are 114 rooms in all, with frescoes of mythological scenes
and landscapes throughout.

Villa Pisani "La Nazionale," Stra, Venice
With this fresco of The Apotheosis of the House of Pisani, painted on the ceiling of the vast ballroom
in 1761-2, Giambattista Tiepolo completed his work in the Veneto, having already employed his
talents on the Villa Volpato, the Villa Soderini (where the frescoes were destroyed in 1917), and the
Palazzina and Foresteria of the Villa Valmarana, known as the Villa of the Dwarfs, in Vicenza.

46

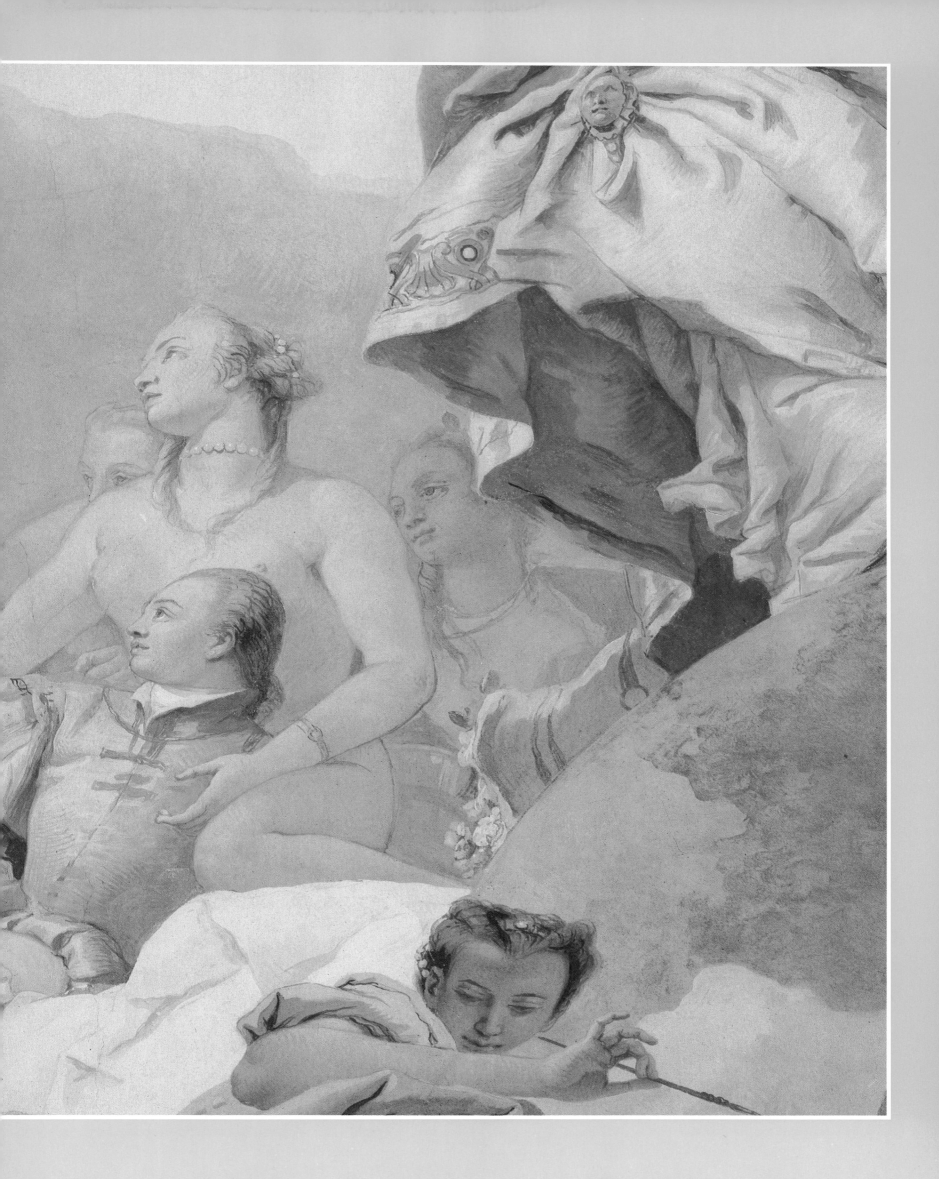

Villa Pisani "La Nazionale," Stra, Venice
At the far end of the garden beyond the long fish pond stand the extraordinary stables, their
majestic splendour befitting the ambitions of a doge such as Alvise Pisani, whose aim was to
outshine other rival households. Designed by Frigimelica, their harmonious proportions are a
marvel of perspective sequence.

Villa Pisani "La Nazionale," Stra, Venice
The spirit of the eighteenth century seems to be crystallized in this maze through which ladies, encumbered by their ample crinolines, gingerly picked their way and, seeing only hedges, called out for help. One can almost hear the animated conversations along the avenues, in the orangery, in the conservatories, in the pavilion surrounded by the fish pond, and in the wood, with its promise of cooling shade.

Villa Pisani "La Barbariga," Stra, Venice
A peaceful view of an eighteenth-century country house, built as a pleasure villa at Stra on the
banks of the Brenta. Chiara Pisani made this the most eloquent example of the aristocratic way of
life in that century, decorating the villa with the richest collection of Venetian stuccowork and
surrounding it with a splendid park in the English style.

Villa Pisani "La Barbariga," Stra, Venice
In the loggias and throughout the park, statues of hunters with their dogs eagerly await the signal
for the shooting party to begin. An atmosphere of nostalgia prevails for the grand hunting parties of
earlier times, as even then the original stables and adjacent farm buildings had already become
purely decorative and places of recreation.

Villa Garzoni, Pontecasale di Candiana, Padua
In the hanging courtyard the light seems to focus on the gentle poses of the statues and on the bright
stone of the Doric arcading which, together with the simpler arcading of the *barchesse* and the
double row of five arches in the façade, create a continuous flow of light and shadow.

Villa Garzoni, Pontecasale di Candiana, Padua
An outstanding example of early air-conditioning. A series of conduits carried water from the
central well, then took it underneath the ground floor to keep the rooms cool in summer. This water
was then channelled outside the building, where it was used to irrigate the garden.

Villa Garzoni, Pontecasale di Candiana, Padua
The hanging courtyard, designed so that the water from the roofs and terraces collects in the gutters
(made of Istrian stone) and runs along a course inside the soffits before converging on the central
well, toward which the slopes of the elaborately patterned courtyard floor also incline.

Villa Contarini, G.E.Ghirardi Foundation, Piazzola sul Brenta, Padua
No villa in the Veneto, not even at the height of the Baroque style, offers such an impressive three-dimensional display of telamons decorating the windows and doorways. These side wings of the villa, which were present on a plan of the site dated 1608, underwent a series of alterations before their almost definitive layout toward the end of the eighteenth century.

Villa Contarini, G.E.Ghirardi Foundation, Piazzola sul Brenta, Padua
Glimpsed through the colonnade supporting the viaduct, this villa has a greater air of unreality than
any other villa in the Veneto, and is undoubtedly one of the most impressive. The central section,
which is unmistakably sixteenth-century (especially the serlianas) was built on the foundations of
an old castle. One theory holds that Palladio himself was the villa's earliest architect.

Villa Contarini, G.E.Ghirardi Foundation, Piazzola sul Brenta, Padua
Antonio Tarsia, one of the greatest eighteenth-century Venetian sculptors, created this line of
elegant statues. Like actors, witnesses to a dazzling period in history, they seem captured in time on
a stage for which the villa itself is the backdrop.

Villa Emo Capodilista, Montecchia di Selvazzano, Padua
Villa Emo is a spectacular sight with its perfectly symmetrical exterior, its remarkable staircase and
Varotari's harmonious series of eight loggias, like the four sides of a crown, providing an
ornamental roof parapet with a strong sense of the theatrical. From north, south, east or west, a
highly functional ramp allowed visitors to reach the villa without having to alight from their carriages.

64

Villa Emo Capodilista, Montecchia di Selvazzano, Padua
Varotari's arrangement of the villa in the form of loggias, and the landscape frescoes with which
they are decorated, create an immediate impression of the harmonious coexistence of external and
internal elements. The ground floor loggias are decorated with pairs of figures representing Adam
and Eve and Venus and Apollo; ornamental grotesques adorn the ceilings.

66

Villa Emo Capodilista, Montecchia di Selvazzano, Padua
Two flights of stone steps set into opposite walls lead to a landing situated midway between ground
and ceiling level at the center of the building. From this landing, two more staircases continue
upward, perpendicular to the first two, creating a singular impression of movement which matches
the curvilinear contour of the walls.

Villa Emo Capodilista, Montecchia di Selvazzano, Padua
Spectacular ceiling decoration in the Sala della Pergola. The cherubs, captured in dynamic pose
along the *trompe l'œil* balustrade of the pergola, or climbing through the leaves, seem almost
caricatures, and reveal the fine expressive talent of the Venetian painter and architect, Varotari.

Villa Emo Capodilista, Montecchia di Selvazzano, Padua
Cherubs on the edge of the balustrade dance all the way round the ceiling, playing with dogs,
parrots and a squirrel on a lead; the foliage provides an impression of refreshing coolness, a
reminder that the villa was designed as a pleasure pavilion and not as a permanent residence.

Petrarch's House, Arquà, Padua
Enchanted by the beauty of the place, Petrarch went to live at Arquà toward the end of his life,
devoting himself to his studies and to writing poetry, and also taking an interest in farming and
agriculture. As a recluse and priest of the culture of Humanism, Petrarch was able to show the
educated classes of the day the model of a working life in close contact with nature.

Petrarch's House, Arquà, Padua
The fresco decorations on the walls of the ground floor, featuring characters from Petrarch's
Canzoniere, would suggest that this part of the house was also lived in. Recurring themes in these
frescoes are the poet's love for Laura, which dominated his life, the struggle between good and evil,
and between the passions and their renunciation.

Petrarch's House, Arquà, Padua
The Camera della Gatta, into which light pours through a curious trefoil arch window, still contains
frescoes from the sixteenth century. Petrarch used these rooms as a study, reading the classics and
continuing his *De viris illustribus* (The lives of illustrious men). The large fireplace, like the loggia,
was added in the sixteenth century.

Petrarch's House, Arquà, Padua

Petrarch's was a modest house, although certainly not spartan in its decoration. The poet
loved to surround himself with things of beauty, as can be seen from the two remaining pieces of
furniture still housed there: the dresser, originally painted in bright red and blue with bronze
knobs, and this richly carved chair of Moorish inspiration.

73

Villa Emo, Rivella, Padua
With the Euganean Hills in the background, a short distance from the Padua to Monselice road
and near the bank of the Battaglia canal, stands the impressive white Palladian-style temple
front portico of Villa Emo. Its lush and verdant surroundings seem unwilling to
reveal the villa's unique beauty, except to a few chosen visitors. Villa Emo was designed by
Vincenzo Scamozzi, architect of the nearby Villa Duodo.

Villa Emo, Rivella, Padua
A striking feature of this villa, in contrast with the simplicity of the rest of the building, is the
sumptuous Corinthian colonnade: it has a high base and terracotta acanthus leaves, a very rare
feature of colonnades in the villas of the Veneto. The evocative setting and the purity of Scamozzi's
architecture make this one of the most beautiful post-Palladian villas of the sixteenth century.

76

Villa Barbarigo, Valsanzibio, Padua
Diana's Bath was originally one of three monumental entrances to the villa. Above a bell-tower
balcony, the goddess, bearing the crescent moon symbol on her head, holds her bow of iron aloft.
On either side of the central arch are high relief hunting trophies and, in the niches, statues of
Endymion and Actaeon. Beneath them, two rustic figures pour barrels of water into the pool.

Villa Barbarigo, Valsanzibio, Padua
The box hedge, specially shaped to create a restful vista, borders the avenue which cuts across the canal like a Roman road as far as the stone stairway, each step of which is inscribed with lines of verse, and then up into the courtyard of the villa with its fountains, balustrades and statues. Each statue has a verse engraved on its pedestal, explaining its significance.

Villa Barbarigo, Valsanzibio, Padua
The fountain of Aeolus and the Rivers, with its cherubs at play with the swans, cuts across the long canal which was originally designed to run from Diana's Bath to an aviary for miniature birds. The water-jets, the fantastic yet harmonious proportions of the park, the labyrinth and the semicircular piazzas make this the jewel of gardens in the Veneto.

Villa dei Vescovi, Luvigliano di Torreglia, Padua
The complex of loggias with its network of connecting staircases seems to rise up unexpectedly, the
warm colour of the brick in marked contrast with the luxuriant natural surroundings. The
landscape filters in with the sunlight through the arcading and its presence is reflected in the
pergolas and vine-shoots decorating the frescoes in the loggias. In the vineyards below the vines are
supported by props cut from chestnut trees, an age-old tradition of the area.

Villa dei Vescovi, Luvigliano di Torreglia, Padua
The Vescovi family's frugality did not extend to the decoration of the only two frescoed rooms.
Despite the influence of his master Titian, the Dutch origin of the fresco painter Lambert Sustris is
evident in his use of light, vivid colours combined with silvery tones. Sustris' idealized landscapes
recall the Euganean Hills in which he worked.

Villa dei Vescovi, Luvigliano di Torreglia, Padua
Restoration of the frescoes carried out between 1965 and 1966 has brought to light all that survives
of an important fresco cycle attributed to Lambert Sustris who painted in Italy during the first half
of the sixteenth century. Around the top of the main hall runs a frieze in which motifs of hunting
trophies alternate with miniature scenes from mythology.

Villa dei Vescovi, Luvigliano di Torreglia, Padua
Panoplies of ancient heroes, insignia and classical symbols are the themes of Mannerist painting,
seen through the eyes of the Dutch artist, Sustris, who trained at the Venetian School, which was
known for its use of radiant colour.

Villa Duodo Cini, Monselice, Padua
Built into the hillside opposite the villa, a broad staircase leading to a walled exedra at the top creates an impressive visual effect and is reminiscent of the classical amphitheater.

Villa Duodo Cini, Monselice, Padua
Scamozzi chose the hill at Monselice as an ideal site for the very wealthy Duodo family's house.
Along the road leading to the villa he built six devotional chapels which, together with the larger
chapel of St. George, were intended to recall the seven basilicas of Rome. Set at regular intervals
and appearing identical at first glance, the chapels in fact vary in architectural order and type.

Villa Giustinian, now Villa Ciani Bassetti V, Roncade, Treviso
The Villa Giustinian is a rare example of the Venetians' presence in the Veneto plain during the
Middle Ages. It is surrounded by the Musestre canal, which at one time was a busy waterway to
and from the lagoon. Over the centuries, the castle has been the subject of many myths and
legends. Nowadays it is used as a center for important cultural events.

Villa Giustinian, now Villa Ciani Bassetti V, Roncade, Treviso
A series of porticos runs along the inside of the castle wall as far as the great towers. Formerly used
for storing corn, they now stand guard over a flourishing wine-producing company, thus restoring
the castle grounds to their original sixteenth-century use, when the small and large gardens were
divided up into vineyard and orchard.

Villa Corner Fiammetta Gabbianelli, Lughignano sul Sile, Treviso
This is one of the most harmoniously proportioned villas along the banks of the River Sile. A map
dating from 1680 provides an idea of the original layout: a fountain stood in front of the villa and to
the east a dovecote; on the river bank was a covered boathouse. The frescoes on the façade are
barely visible, although traces of cherubs riding sea-horses remain in one part and, in another,
acanthus plant volutes interrupted by monochrome caryatids supporting the window sills.

Villa Cornaro, Piombino Dese, Padua
Proportion, elegance and formality characterize the design of this villa, which is a compromise between a town and a country house. The central Ionic portico and Corinthian loggia create an impression of space and light, the play of shadows behind the pristine columns creating visual echoes against the rusticated stonework walls which are pierced by modest windows.

Villa Cornaro, Piombino Dese, Padua
The statues in the main hall of Catherine Cornaro, Queen of Cyprus, and of her ill-fated husband,
Giacomo di Lusignano, are by Camillo Mariani. At her house, Altivole, in Asolo, no trace remains
of the beautiful portrait, attributed to Giorgione, of the queen on a white horse at a deer hunt. The
painting used to hang over the main entrance which was demolished in the nineteenth century.

Villa Cornaro, Piombino Dese, Padua
View across the garden, surrounded by flower beds and fish ponds. The farm buildings near the
villa appear in a seventeenth-century drawing in which a dovecote provides a central feature. Villa
Cornaro has been one of the most imitated examples of Palladian architecture: since the late
seventeenth century it has been used as a model by British and American architects in particular,
Inigo Jones being among the most prolific exponents.

101

Villa Marcello, Levada di Piombino Dese, Padua
A vast and strictly symmetrical Italian garden provides the setting for this eighteenth-century villa.
Inside, a lively colour scheme of green, pink and yellow echoes the colours of Venice in the
eighteenth-century lacquerware and in the wall decorations. In the main hall is a fine Venetian or
terrazzo floor – marble chips set in cement, ground smooth and then polished.

Villa Marcello, Levada di Piombino Dese, Padua
Campaspe in Apelles' studio, one of the frescoes by Giambattista Crosato in the impressive two-storey hall, where a perfect balance has been achieved between the painting and architectural features. Crosato was a leading painter and scenographer, and his finest work was the decoration of the Palazzina di Stupinigi in Turin.

Villa Marcello, Levada di Piombino Dese, Padua
Also by Crosato is this fresco commemorating the wedding of Alexander and Roxana, from the
cycle of stories about the life of Alexander the Great. In these frescoes, which date from 1734,
Crosato reveals the importance of luminous colour, characteristic of the Venetian School; to it he
adds the technique he learned at the court of Savoy of applying paint to a porous surface in order to
increase its brilliance.

Villa Rinaldi, Casella d'Asolo, Treviso
This villa dates originally from the late sixteenth century. Since then it has undergone a number of modifications which have all contributed to the effect of a spacious and animated stage set, not least because of the villa's unique location at the foot of the Asolo hills, which are steeped in history.

Villa Rinaldi, Casella d'Asolo, Treviso
Simple mythological themes and tricks of perspective characterize the decorations by Pietro Liberi
and Andrea Celesti, visually increasing the interior space through the devices of architectural
elements and landscapes, both real and *trompe l'œil*.

Villa Rinaldi, Casella d'Asolo, Treviso
The contrast of the actual architecture mirrored in *trompe l'œil* representations of it create an
extraordinary visual effect: the spatial imagination seems infinite as the real space appears to be
enclosed by more magnificent and fantastic imaginary sets. Painted columns on one side reflect the
real columns opposite, creating a spectacular effect of shifting reality.

Villa Rinaldi, Casella d'Asolo, Treviso
The particular setting of this villa at the foot of the hills and the intimate rapport between its
architecture and the features of the natural surroundings achieve a perfectly harmonious balance.
In the gardens and in niches, statues of characters from Ariosto's epic *Orlando Furioso* seem to
revive the heroic spirit of the poem and the period.

112

Villa Barbaro, Maser, Treviso
Simple, basic and perfectly symmetrical, the façade, which is divided into three sections, is
reminiscent of the houses overlooking the canals in Venice. In siting the villa on the slope of the hill,
Palladio has produced a model construction which blends harmoniously with the surrounding landscape.

114

Villa Barbaro, Maser, Treviso
The frescoed ceiling in the Hall of the Tribunal of Love. The bride stands before the judge with the
allegories of Justice and Truth; the jubilant cherubs are celebrating the happy verdict. Below, on
either side of the hearth of Victory, two allegorical figures of Toil and Peace look down on an
exhortation in Latin not to take up arms.

116

Villa Barbaro, Maser, Treviso
The Hall of Bacchus. In the ceiling vault, the figure of Bacchus animates the whole scene by the turning movement of his body. Bacchus is offering grapes to mortals, his gesture made the more persuasive by sweet music provided by young maidens, the overall effect enhanced by the swirling clouds in the background. Below, the mantelpiece by Alessandro Vittoria bears the legend in praise of spontaneity: "do not conceal the fire in your breast."

Villa Barbaro, Maser, Treviso
Human and divine elements are combined in this fresco by Paolo Veronese. On the balcony,
between huge white spiral columns, are the figures of Giustiniana Barbaro – the mistress of the
house, together with the old wet-nurse – and a young boy, identified as her third child. These
figures seem to stand out from the background, an effect which is heightened by the difference in
perspective and also by the bold brushstrokes.

Villa Barbaro, Maser, Treviso
A detail of the cruciform hall, where figures of female musicians perform in praise of Harmony. The
trompe l'oeil effect of doors and people is extremely convincing. The figure on the right, a
personification of folk music, is resting her foot on what is either a rare instrument or a container in
which to keep spare strings; the long rectangular instrument she is holding is the stringed
tambourine which was much used at the time.

Villa Barbaro, Maser, Treviso

Through the Hall of Olympus, at the end of a long enfilade and framed in a false doorway, stands a huntsman, possibly Veronese himself, who was thirty years old at the time. The visual effect is heightened by the succession of colour contrasts from one door frame to the next. Veronese took particular delight in combining legends he had created for the ceilings with episodes from daily life in the villa, yet without affecting the unity of the whole.

Villa Barbaro, Maser, Treviso
Detail of the façade. The centerpiece of the heraldic tympanum, the work of Vittoria, is an allegory
of the Barbaro family: two marine deities astride strange dolphins are carrying off water nymphs.
Above a bucranium, or ox's head, is the two-headed eagle of the Empire, the Barbaro insignia. The
balcony connects the perfect proportions of the interior with the sweep of the land sloping down to
Neptune's fountain.

122

Villa Barbaro, Maser, Treviso
The dovecote and sundial on the southeastern side of the villa. "There are Galleries on both sides of
the House, at the end of which are two Pigeon-houses; and below them are the presses for the
Vintage with the Stable and other necessary places for Husbandry." (Palladio, *I Quattro Libri
dell'Architettura*, book II, ch. XIV, Venice, 1570).

Villa Barbaro, Maser, Treviso
Behind the villa, this broad nymphaeum encircling the fish pond is decorated with large telamons
and crowned with a statue of Diana, with water piped from a spring on the hillside above spouting
from her breasts. The walls are adorned with mythological and allegorical figures amid panoplies,
bucrania and festoons of fruit. The central grotto, deep in shadow, is dedicated to Neptune and was
built by Vittoria.

Villa Emo, Fanzolo di Vedelago, Treviso
The portico has the perfect proportions of a small tetrastyle Tuscan Doric temple. The slope in front
replaces a more formal flight of steps, creating an impression of distance. The modern layout of the
garden, with the addition of statues, resulted from an eighteenth-century redrawing of the
boundaries of the land which isolated the villa from the village.

Villa Emo, Fanzolo di Vedelago, Treviso
This villa, with its arcaded *barchesse*, projects into the surrounding country and dominates the land.
The central block stands out on an extended area of paved ground, marking the center of an axis,
flanked by avenues of trees, which provides a link between the open country and the village
beyond.

127

Villa Emo, Fanzolo di Vedelago, Treviso
The beauty of this villa lies almost exclusively in the unity of its proportions and in the contrast
between open and closed spaces. The building responded perfectly to the requirements of the
original commission, achieving a finely judged match between the ideal "country court"
architecture and the elaborate decor of the interior.

Villa Emo, Fanzolo di Vedelago, Treviso
Allegory of fire or prophetic divination in grotesques by Zelotti. Two supplicant soothsayers
question the spirit of a dead man emanating from the flame on the altar. This soul, in the form of a
bronze statue, appears on the pediment of the temple, the head in profile against a white circle from
which hang festoons of fruit tied to the malignant red sorghum plant. Incense burns to dispel the
stench from the Harpies who are attempting to steal the responsories.

Villa Emo, Fanzolo di Vedelago, Treviso
In the room dedicated to the Arts, decorated with frescoes by Zelotti, the Arts are personified by six
beautiful women, while Amphyon, to the sound of a lyre, moves stones to build Thebes. Sculpture
is depicted carving a statue, and Poetry (above) points out in an open book the exact point at which
the visitor is standing.

131

Villa Emo, Fanzolo di Vedelago, Treviso
The loggia is decorated with frescoes relating the loves of Callisto and Jupiter (disguised as Diana), together with Juno avenging her betrayal, and the transfiguration of the nymph into a propitious star to Fertility, personified by Ceres and visible above the entrance. The coffered ceiling, divided into nine sections, is a replica of the original, and the reconstruction retains the original fascias, frescoed with ram and festoon motifs. The high relief in the tympanum with the family coat-of-arms is by Vittoria.

Villa Emo, Fanzolo di Vedelago, Treviso
This doorway incorporates a frescoed tympanum and allegorical figures of Prudence and Plenty.
The ceiling of the vestibule is decorated with a pergola of vines. In the main hall beyond is the great
orchestration of Zelotti's frescoes in which, between Corinthian columns, scenes from classical
mythology are depicted together with monochrome figures representing the Four Elements,
prisoners, and trophies.

La Rocca Pisana, Lonigo, Vicenza
An original design by Scamozzi and almost impenetrable in appearance, the Rocca Pisana consists of a circular central hall with four large corner niches contained within a square outer structure. Unlike the Rotonda, whose four porticos extend beyond the façade on each side, this has only one portico, which is recessed within the main entrance façade. On each of the remaining façades is a single Serlian arcade.

La Rocca Pisana, Lonigo, Vicenza
The remarkable ground floor of the Rocca Pisana, with the shadows cast by the low vaulted
ceilings, is reminiscent of a secret medieval crypt; muted daylight filters into the very center of the
villa through the openwork grille. Light rebounds off the vaulted ceilings of the passageways,
enhancing the clear-cut profiles of the white stone pilasters.

La Rocca Pisana, Lonigo, Vicenza
The plan of the ground floor is circular; four square pilasters support its powerful central structure
and mark the boundaries of an aperture covered by an openwork grille. This is situated in the floor
of the hall above, directly below the eye of the dome overhead, and forms the lower pole of the
central axis of the building.

La Rocca Pisana, Lonigo, Vicenza
To the left and right of the east and west corridors Scamozzi designed a stairwell for two identical
spiral staircases: these are stark and functional, the stone steps spiralling upward around the slender
pillar which forms an axis through the center of the stairwell.

La Rocca Pisana, Lonigo, Vicenza
An impressive sense of space is created in the central hall by the very high open dome. The great
niches reflect the light which pours in from above and through the Serlian arcade. The plainness of
the stone walls enhances the interplay of shape and form of the oval and rectangular small
windows, and of the hemispherical banded stone ribs and circular aperture of the dome above.

Villa Capra "La Rotonda," Vicenza
"Today I visited the splendid building which stands on a pleasant elevation about half a league
from the town, and is called the "Rotonda." . . . Probably the luxury of architecture was never
carried to so high a point . . . And while the building appears in all its magnificence, when viewed
from any spot in the district, it also forms the point of view for a most agreeable prospect."
(Goethe *Travels in Italy*, 1816–17)

Villa Capra "La Rotonda," Vicenza

Frescoed by Alessandro Maganza, a pupil of Fasolo, the great dome in the main hall is divided by stucco ornamentation into four sections. The imposing female figures, almost awkwardly clothed in their drapes, include Temperance; Chastity, in reluctant pose; Justice; the beautiful nude figure of Fame; Prudence astride an elephant; and Faith kneeling before an altar. The statues in front of the niches, and the stucco decorations are by Agostino Rubini.

142

Villa Capra "La Rotonda," Vicenza
From the main central hall four corridors radiate out of the villa to each of the porticos. These
corridors divide the whole building into four parts, each of which has a hall and a room next to the
staircase. Stairs then connect the *piano nobile* to a corresponding layout of rooms on the floors
above and below. The powerful gods of Olympus, in frescoes by Dorigny, suggest an almost
rhetorical eloquence.

144

Villa Capra "La Rotonda," Vicenza
This grotesque face of a faun with a contemptuous smile was undoubtedly modelled on an existing
Roman relief. Situated directly beneath the central opening of the dome, it served to drain the rain
water in the same way as the impluvium in a Roman house.

Villa Pisani, Bagnolo di Lonigo, Vicenza
The result of Palladio's first encounter with the world of Venetian patronage was this building in
celebration of the landowning Pisani family. The villa was originally ideally situated to
communicate its message of architectural lyricism, though the subsequent erection of an
embankment along the river's edge obscured the east view from the house.

147

Villa Pisani, Bagnolo di Lonigo, Vicenza
The lunette window in the vault of the cruciform main hall was designed to illuminate the interior;
an identical feature was to have been included in the façade overlooking the River Guà, but the
tympanum on that side replaced Palladio's original idea. Now daylight enters the villa through the
main entrance and side windows. The harmonious fresco decoration of the vaulted ceiling is the
work of an unknown sixteenth-century artist.

Villa Pojana, Pojana Maggiore, Vicenza
Designed by Palladio, the villa departs from the master architect's stereotypes in the addition of the
Serlian opening to the entrance: the arched doorway, flanked by two smaller apertures on either
side, interrupts the clear-cut simplicity of line in the smooth surface of the wall, creating a
distinctive chiaroscuro effect. The statue to the right of the entrance steps is by Girolamo Albanese.

Villa Pojana, Pojana Maggiore, Vicenza
The interior arched doorway with the broad circular cornice surmounting it, and the five "eyes" or
oculi spanning the semicircle of stone. The monumental effect of the interior is an unexpected
surprise: the villa is magnificent and splendidly proportioned. The central ceiling is a cross vault;
the adjacent side room has barrel vault ceilings. The frescoes are attributed to Bernardino India.

151

Villa Pojana, Pojana Maggiore, Vicenza
This scene of a sacrifice in a fresco by Anselmo Canera in the Hall of the Emperors depicts the
oldest member of the Pojana family leading his people in the extinguishing of the flame of discord
on the altar of peace. Canera's gifted use of colour is clearly demonstrated in the medallions in the
central hall, which are in the style of Veronese.

Villa Conti Lampertico, "La Deliziosa," Montegaldella, Vicenza
Close to the River Bacchiglione stands "La Deliziosa," its white portico proportioned by the giant
Ionic order of two columns and two corner pilasters; the statues on the roof belong to the original
seventeenth-century plan, and not to the radical nineteenth-century "remodernization" of the villa.

Villa Conti Lampertico "La Deliziosa," Montegaldella, Vicenza
There is a refreshing liveliness and immediate spontaneity in the elegant movements of the dance
which seems to absorb its rhythm and cadence from the merry ensemble of these able musicians;
throughout the gardens an air of composed and ironic participation in events, destined to continue
for ever, transcends the human scale of the physical surroundings.

Villa Conti Lampertico "La Deliziosa," Montegaldella, Vicenza
The gates to the gardens of this villa are in wrought ironwork of the highest quality; the gardens
once contained 164 statues, among which are the Commedia dell'Arte characters sculpted by
Orazio Marinali. A highly talented artist in an age of increased theatrical awareness, Marinali's
greatest champion was the eighteenth-century Venetian playwright Goldoni.

155

Villa-castle Grimani Marcello, Montegalda, Vicenza
A view of the upper garden, reached by passing through a finely crafted wrought-iron gate which is reminiscent of the intricate work of the gates at "La Deliziosa." A narrow avenue, flanked by lemon trees, divides the formal Italian-style garden, which commands an impressive view of the surrounding countryside.

Villa-castle Grimani Marcello, Montegalda, Vicenza
Rows of tall cypresses surround the base of the majestic castle, visible for miles around on its
imposing hilltop. The towers of the old turreted villa-castle make a unique spectacle as they
dominate the plain of the Veneto below. The inner courtyard, with statues by Marinali above and
below, draws the eye to the battlements beyond.

Villa Godi, Lonedo di Lugo, Vicenza
There is an austere, serious, almost closed atmosphere about this villa, as though the central section
is compressed by the side wings. This was one of Palladio's earliest projects, and the later hallmark
of his style can be seen in embryo here. Designed before his journey to Rome, it is expressive of a
culture based on models in the Veneto, where the "voice" of Sanmicheli sounded with particular
authority. In front of the villa are two finely proportioned hanging gardens.

158

Villa Godi, Lonedo di Lugo, Vicenza
The far wall of the main hall, where Corinthian columns support the tympanum, at either end of
which is a superbly detailed figure of a reclining woman. In the center, the charismatic figure of
"Fame" sits above two prisoners. Zelotti's vivid use of colour, at its peak of perfection here, is
continued in the dazzling breastplates featured among the feats of arms depicted on the main walls.

Villa Godi, Lonedo di Lugo, Vicenza
Gualtiero Padovano and his assistants painted the frescoes in the loggia which overlooks the gentle
surrounding landscape and which, together with the central main hall, divides the *piano nobile*
symmetrically in two. Padovano, Zelotti and Battista del Moro, all of whom worked on the frescoes,
were praised by Palladio as "the most individual and excellent of painters."

Villa Godi, Lonedo di Lugo, Vicenza
In the Room of the Muses, these magnificent, in some ways ungainly, caryatids use their strong
arms to support the beam, above which runs a frieze featuring cherubs, bucrania and busts: in
contrast with the grey tone of the caryatids, this peaceful scene of the Muses and Poets, is painted in
light and delicate colours. These paintings are possibly the work of Battista del Moro.

164

Villa Godi, Lonedo di Lugo, Vicenza
Bacchus and two deities in the Room of Olympus. A superb example of plasticity in representing the
male nude, demonstrating the sensitivity and power of portrayal close to that of a sculptor, although
Zelotti never achieves Veronese's effects of pure light; violet tints illuminated by flickerings of white
are a characteristic feature of Zelotti's work.

165

Villa da Porto Colleoni, Thiene, Vicenza
Evocative in the twilight, the Gothic five-light window marks the exact center of this harmoniously proportioned façade. Six carved roses directly above the marble mullions contribute to the elaborate detail. Above is a line of Ghibelline battlements, outlined in relief; from this point the roof extends to the towers above, with their five Ghibelline merlons.

Villa da Porto Colleoni, Thiene, Vicenza
This study of Pallas Athene and Mercury above the door in the south wall, like the Venus and
Vulcan beside the hearth, would appear to be the work of Zelotti; however, the exquisite shaping of
the legs, the softness and freshness of the flesh-tones in the figure of Mercury, and Athene's plumed
helmet and shield show a degree of fineness unfamiliar in Zelotti's work.

167

Villa da Porto Colleoni, Thiene, Vicenza
The Clemency of Scipio, by Antonio Fasolo and Giambattista Zelotti. Motivated by the inspiration
of Roman times, Zelotti has created figures of enormous expressive force while confronting the
problem of adapting a majestic vision to what are modest rooms compared with the vast halls of a
prince's palace.

Villa da Porto Colleoni, Thiene, Vicenza
Antony and Cleopatra at a banquet, painted by Fasolo. The powerful face of the Roman leader has
been rendered with such strength of line and expressive intensity as to suggest the genuine portrait
of a historical figure in whom Fasolo may have chosen to immortalize the likeness of his patron.

Villa da Porto Colleoni, Thiene, Vicenza
The splendid eighteenth-century stables are attributed to Francesco Muttoni. Each stall is separated
by richly carved partitions and by columns on which the harnesses were hung. An artificial water-
course still runs beneath these stables; the water was used for cleaning the horses, which were led
into the circle in the foreground. This position benefited from maximum daylight which flooded in
through the open side doors.

170

Villa Della Torre, Fumane, Verona

Once described as the most magnificent villa around Verona and, indeed, the richest in the whole of
Italy for its gardens, fountains, the villa itself, its outbuildings and orchard, which all blend perfectly
with the natural surroundings, the Villa Della Torre is now enjoying a new period of splendour as a
result of restoration work carried out by the Cazzola family. The original architect, either Romano
or Sanmicheli, included a peristyle reminiscent of those found in ancient Roman houses.

Villa Della Torre, Fumane, Verona
One of four stupendous hearth masks in the villa: this decoration marks a fresh exploration of
terrific motifs, enhanced by the kind of amusing irony often found in garden statuary, but unusual
as a fireplace surround.

Villa Serego, Santa Sofia di San Pietro in Cariano, Verona
"Its situation is on a very fine Hill of a most easy ascent, between two Vallies, from whence one sees a great part of the City. Round about are several other Hills very agreeable to the Eye, and abounding with excellent Waters, whereby the House and Garden are adorn'd with several admirable Fountains." (Palladio, *I Quattro Libri dell'Architettura*, book II, ch. XV, Venice 1570).

Villa Serego, Santa Sofia di San Pietro in Cariano, Verona
Part of the ground-floor colonnade, whose massive Ionic columns create extraordinary effects of
light and shade. Constructed of large sections of rusticated ashlar set one on top of the other, each
column bears an incorporated pilaster with capital on the inner side, which supports the architraves
of the upper loggia. This villa was the last in Palladio's long and prolific series of "country houses."

Villa Serego, Santa Sofia di San Pietro in Cariano, Verona
A number of stone sculptures were placed in the gardens of the villa during the eighteenth century.
This excellently sculpted figure of Atlas, kneeling and supporting a stone bowl on his shoulders
instead of the sky, is in keeping with the traditional hunchbacked figures or holy water stoups
commonly found in many churches in Verona.

Villa Allegri Arvedi, Cuzzano di Grezzana, Verona
Enjoying an outstanding position in close harmony with the natural surroundings, this villa now retains only some of the features which, in the eighteenth century, made it a perfect example of a working farm villa, such as the steward's office, the stables, the olive oil-works, the tobacco drying rooms, the ironing-room for the laundry, the fishery for keeping live fish, the "glacery" for ice-making, and, in the orchard, the fine net or large aviary for decoy birds.

Villa Allegri Arvedi, Cuzzano di Grezzana, Verona
Still life frescoes by Falezza, painted with great spontaneity and luminosity of colour, decorate the
right-hand tower of the villa. The background presents a general view of the villa, with a jay flying
overhead. The wooden ceiling provides a scene of great activity with a wide variety of birds,
including chaffinch, thrush, titmice, a bright-eyed owl and a woodpecker, busy at work among the
boughs and foliage.

Villa Allegri Arvedi, Cuzzano di Grezzana, Verona
A splendid example of an Italian-style garden, dating from the latter half of the eighteenth century,
possibly to a design by Giovanni Battista Bianchi who was also responsible for the construction of
the villa. An eighteenth-century print by Volkamer shows the villa on a raised site with an
extravagance of box-hedge topiary and a central fountain.

182

Villa Allegri Arvedi, Cuzzano di Grezzana, Verona
The powerful stance of Dorigny's figures leads the eye through the doors to the fertile countryside
beyond. The densely wooded hillside behind the villa slopes down to the thickets of cypresses that
surround the elegant Baroque chapel dedicated to San Carlo.

Villa Allegri Arvedi, Cuzzano di Grezzana, Verona
Immutable witness to the changes that have taken place over the centuries, this statue focuses the
eye on the geometric shapes and sinuous lines of the hedges and gardens, as their gentle patterns
extend toward the outline of the nearby hills.

185

Villa Badoer, Fratta Polesine, Rovigo
An impression of movement is created by the diverging lines of the semicircular open galleries
surrounding much of the garden, and the steps leading up to the villa, and linking it to these
porticos. The heraldic coat-of-arms of the Mocenigo family is the only decoration in the tympanum.
The sense of motion is further heightened by the contrast between the light walls and the red
terracotta paving stones.

The villas

Villa Barbaro
MASER

Villa Rinaldi
CASELLA D'ASOLO

CONEGLIANO

Villa Godi
LONEDO DI LUGO

BASSANO

MONTEBELLUNA

PORTOGRUARO

SCHIO

Villa da Porto Colleoni
THIENE

Villa Emo
FANZOLO

TREVISO

Villa Marcello
LEVADA

Villa Giustinian
RONCADE

CASTELFRANCO VENETO

Villa Corner Fiammetta
LUGHIGNANO

S. DONÀ DI PIAVE

VICENZA

Villa Cornaro
PIOMBINO DESE

Villa Contarini
PIAZZOLA SUL BRENTA

ZIANIGO

BARDOLINO

Villa Della Torre
FUMANE

Villa Allegri Arvedi
CUZZANO DI GREZZANA

La Rotonda
VICENZA

Villa Serego
SAN PIETRO IN CARIANO

MONTECCHIO MAGGIORE

Castello Grimani
MONTEGALDA

Villa Foscari
MALCONTENTA

MURANO

VERONA

La Deliziosa
MONTEGALDELLA

Villa Emo Capodilista
MONTECCHIA DI SELVAZZANO

Villa Pisani
La Barbariga
STRA

MIRA

VENICE

La Rocca Pisana
LONIGO

Villa Pisani
BAGNOLO DI LONIGO

PADUA

Villa dei Vescovi
LUVIGLIANO DI TORREGLIA

Villa Pojana
POJANA

Villa Barbarigo
VALSANZIBIO

Villa Emo
RIVELLA

Petrarch's House
ARQUÀ

Villa Duodo Cini
MONSELICE

Villa Garzoni
PONTECASALE DI CANDIANA

ESTE

ROVIGO

Villa Badoer
FRATTA POLESINE

Lake Garda

Tesina

Bacchiglione

Brenta

Piave

Sile

Livenza

Adige

Po

The **Villa Foscari** at Malcontenta, often incorrectly called "La Malcontenta," was designed by Palladio (1508–80) for Niccolò and Luigi Foscari and built between 1550 and 1560; the exact date is not known. Its fresco decoration, begun by Battista Franco (1498–1561) and continued by Giambattista Zelotti (1526–78), was probably brought to completion by 1567. The villa stands on the edge of the Brenta, not far from Venice, and was frequently visited by the Serenissima's most illustrious guests. Henri III of France came with Emanuele Filiberto, Duke of Savoy, in 1574; two other elected kings of Poland visited the villa at the end of the seventeenth and early in the eighteenth century while the King of Denmark, Frederick IV, was a guest there in 1709.

The temple front portico of the canal façade consists of six Ionic columns executed in brick and is one of Palladio's most superbly harmonious creations. The architect himself speaks of the tall basement on which it is set and also alludes to the way in which he continued its cornice around the entire house as a frieze. Originally the basement also had an extension in two walls, enclosing gardens at either side of the house. However, the basement was not intended as a merely aesthetic element. It raised the *piano nobile* 11 ft (3.6 m) above the damp marshy ground, safely out of reach of the Brenta's occasional flooding while providing the house with kitchen, service and storage space on the ground floor.

The front door leads from the portico directly into the great vaulted main hall, lit by three large windows crowned with a lunette borrowed from the Roman baths of classical antiquity. Palladio's description of the villa's interior in the *Quattro Libri* dwells on the height and vaulting of this and the lower side rooms, revealing his persistent fascination with the varied interior elevations of the Roman baths. The published plan of the villa illustrates an equally persistent concern with mathematical proportion that sometimes seems almost obsessive. The smallest side room measures 12 × 16 Venetian feet; the next is 16 × 16, while the largest and, incidentally, the tallest of the series of three is 16 × 24. The basic module of four is continued in the great hall which is 32 feet wide and almost 48 feet long, while the plan makes it clear that the size of the portico and even the spacing of the columns was meant to be included in this extraordinary programme. Professor Wittkower has likened all of this to theories of musical harmony derived from Pythagoras and a classical setting was certainly what the Foscari sought in the fresco decoration of the interior.

The house followed the vicissitudes of the Venetian Republic and was only rescued from dereliction after the First World War by Mr Albert Landsberg. He had the walls cleaned of the whitewash that had been applied when the villa served as a military hospital. The great villa on the Brenta at Malcontenta is once again the property of the Foscari family who, in the present generation, have continued the work of restoration and preservation begun by Mr Landsberg.

The Villa Pisani at Stra was begun in 1736 on designs by Francesco Maria Preti (1701 – 74) to celebrate the election the previous year of Alvise Pisani as the one-hundred-and-fourteenth Doge of the Venetian Republic. Preti's vast edifice was actually the third villa to occupy this site on the banks of the River Brenta in the eighteenth century. The original seventeenth-century house was demolished early on to make way for a new villa and for a series of elaborate outbuildings planned by the Paduan architect Girolamo Frigimelica (1653 – 1732), who had long been at work on the immense palace under construction in Venice for the Pisani family. By the time of Frigimelica's death in 1732, several of his projects on the estate had been completed, including the extraordinary stable block. Its long and imposing façade, crowned with a panoply of gesticulating statues and preceded by a giant portico of six great Ionic columns masks a building containing twenty-four stalls for the Pisani horses. Frigimelica's gateways and belvederes, scattered throughout the park, are a triumph of motifs borrowed from classical architecture and assembled in the richly eclectic style of eighteenth-century Baroque taste.

The builder's wooden model of the villa itself still survives and also testifies to the exuberant Baroque style of Frigimelica's architecture. However, after the architect's death, the building must have seemed old-fashioned, if not inadequate to the Pisani and when Alvise Pisani was elected Doge, the decision was taken to demolish this building as well and to begin again on an even grander scale.

Preti's Villa Pisani took twenty years to complete and is undoubtedly the largest and most impressive villa ever built in the Veneto. The architecture could be described as neo-Palladian, so prominent are the elements derived from sixteenth-century prototypes. The central block is a wide, temple front portico rendered in bas-relief, like the façade of the Villa Barbaro at Maser, with half columns capped in the rich Corinthian order. The garland-bearing putti in the frieze above come from Sansovino's Libreria Marciana which Palladio had called "the richest building since classical antiquity." The ground floor façade is even richer, with giant caryatids like those also created for the Marciana by the sculptor Alessandro Vittoria (1525 – 1608), Palladio's collaborator at Maser.

The high base of the villa at Stra supports a *piano nobile* which rises, in the central block, through an upper mezzanine floor. The windows of this upper half floor light a balcony that completely encircles the great central hall of the villa. To crown this vast two-storey space, the Pisani commissioned Giambattista Tiepolo (1696 – 1770) to paint the *Gloria di Casa Pisani* (The Apotheosis of the House of Pisani) in a framework designed by Gerolamo Mengozzi Colonna (1688–1772), a masterpiece of *trompe l'œil* architecture in fresco. In Tiepolo's gigantic celestial tableau, painted between 1761 and 1762, Venice accompanies the Pisani to their apotheosis before the figure of Power. They are surrounded by the Arts and allegories of peace under the Virgin's protection, while Fame trumpets their greatness to the four corners of the Earth. But although the fame of the Pisani has been perpetuated in this artistic masterpiece – the last work painted by Tiepolo before his departure for Spain – their power and that of Venice itself were soon eclipsed and in 1807 the villa was acquired by the Emperor Napoleon, who spent the night there on November 29. He in turn bestowed the great building, now a royal palace rather than a pleasure villa, on his stepson and viceroy, Eugène de Beauharnais, whom he had created an Imperial Highness named the Prince of Venice. From then the villa followed the fate of the nation, belonging in turn to the emperors of Austria and then to the kings of Italy. Almost precisely two hundred years after the election of Alvise Pisani that had inspired this last great expression of the power and wealth of the Venetian patriciate, the Villa Pisani became a stage for one of the dramas of recent European history: it was the setting for Mussolini and Hitler's first meeting on 12 July 1934.

The exceptionally long ivy-covered façade of the Villa Pisani, known as **La Barbariga** (from the marriage of Chiara Pisani with Filippo Barbarigo) presents the harmonious image of an eighteenth-century country house built for pleasure on the banks of the Brenta at Stra. However, in the eighteenth century the villa turned its back to the river that had become known as the *strada dei capricci* because of the rich variety of pleasure villas that sprang up in what Goldoni satirized as the *smanie di villeggiatura*, the mania for villa holidays. The front of the house now faced a vast park laid out in the latest English fashion by Chiara Pisani Barbarigo. The villa reveals its diverse origins and complicated architectural history on the garden side. The simple, original central block was embellished during the eighteenth century with two extraordinary *barchessa* wings that seem a curious compendium of every style of architecture from sixteenth-century Mannerism to the latest neo-Classical fashion. The triangular pediments in the center of each *barchessa* make these outbuildings far more imposing than the villa itself and since each *barchessa* is raised up on steps, it is clear that the original stable block or farm building function has been abandoned in favour of purely ornamental considerations.

Ornament is certainly the key theme in the interior of the villa where the rooms provide one of the most splendid displays of eighteenth-century Venetian stuccowork to be seen anywhere in the Veneto. The space over doors and the long walls of each room enclose framing motifs executed in the double curves beloved of rococo *ébanistes* and cabinet-makers. Each frond and cartouche is modelled in a free form impasto of plaster without benefit of moulds, while stuccowork vines and leaves weave themselves in and out of the ornament. A highly carved and gilt-framed mirror hangs like an oval medallion against the plain white center of the wall, while similar shapes appear repeated in plasterwork motifs that enliven the flat ceilings. The delicate rococo frivolity of one room finds an echo in the chinoiserie fantasy of the next, where spindly palm trees or pagodas provide the backdrop to exotic plaster figures in flowing robes and coolie hats. The Pisani were important patrons of sculptors as well as stuccadors and the villa houses a plastercast copy of the famous *Three Graces*, executed by the family's erstwhile protégé Antonio Canova (1757 – 1822) for Napoleon's Empress in 1813. An even earlier generation of Venetian sculpture is represented in the splendid series of life-size stone statues of the Pisani's eighteenth-century gamekeepers and their dogs which now line the colonnade of the villa's *barchessa*.

The **Villa Garzoni** at Pontecasale, situated only 15½ miles (25 km) due west of the Venetian lagoon's southernmost point, is a monument to the link between the architecture of Venice's golden age in the sixteenth century and the evolution of the villa in the Veneto. The Garzoni were a recently ennobled banking family who had undertaken the arduous task of land reclamation in this marshy district, almost seventy-five years before Francesco Garzoni commissioned Jacopo Sansovino (1486 – 1570) to build a great villa in the midst of their estates. Sansovino's project for the Garzoni is generally accepted as contemporary with his work on the Libreria Marciana in Venice between 1537 and 1550. Although simple and unadorned by contrast with that extravaganza of triumphalism in urban public building, the Villa Garzoni displays elements borrowed from every phase of Sansovino's training. Perhaps the most successful was his use of the Doric bay, borrowed from the Theater of Marcellus, built in Rome's Augustan period. The arcade of round-arched openings separated by half columns on square bases, rising to support a cornice above the arches, became a widespread motif in European architecture, but in Sansovino's day it had been only tentatively employed by architects of the early Renaissance. Only Falconetto in the Veneto had used the motif before Sansovino and his version at the Villa dei Vescovi depended more on its colouristic and decorative possibilities than on its architectonic elements.

Both the Villa dei Vescovi and the Villa Garzoni were built on raised platforms or basements. Falconetto resorted to this device to compensate for the hilly site at Luvigliano, but at Pontecasale Sansovino had another intention. The platform conceals a true, vault-supported basement containing dark, cavernous storerooms. The villa was built above, but not in a solid block like Falconetto's creation. It rises from the edge of the platform only on three sides leaving a large open-ended courtyard in the center of the platform. The stone slab pavement of this courtyard, laid in a broad pattern, slopes away from an elaborately carved stone wellhead in the center. The rainwater that drains from the courtyard falls into a cistern built in the basement area under the courtyard, while the upper well-head is little more than an opening through which the real well below can be reached.

The U-shaped building is two storeys high while the broad terrace overlooking the courtyard surrounds it on all four sides. The courtyard façades of the upper floor are undecorated; in contrast, the terrace is not only populated with statues but is also supported on a Doric arcade that is one of the most handsome passages of High Renaissance architecture in a Veneto villa.

Sansovino gave a much more severe and simple arcading to the nearby outbuildings – barchesse built outside the precinct of the villa's walled garden forecourt – but on the sides facing the villa he designed triumphal arch gateways, executed in brick and framed with motifs taken from the most sophisticated sources, such as Sebastiano Serlio and Giulio Romano. In this almost palatial vein, Sansovino designed caryatid-supported chimney hoods for two of the ground floor rooms and a suite of walnut furniture, some of which is now in the Cini Collection, including a tall armoire ornamented with well-muscled caryatids, probably carved by the sculptor-architect himself. Much of the statuary on the property may be contemporary with the building and the two giant statues of the Labours of Hercules on the entrance staircase have been interpreted as part of an allegorical programme alluding to the Garzoni's century-long labours to reclaim and cultivate the lands of Pontecasale.

The **Villa Contarini** at Piazzola sul Brenta, not far from Padua, has as rich and complicated a history as any monument built in Venetian territory. The vast Piazzola estates came into the Contarini family through marriage in 1413 at a time when Padua had only recently submitted to the Serenissima and the Republic could at long last regulate and control the course of the River Brenta which had been the most profitable, if frequently contested, commercial link between Padua and the Venetian lagoon ever since the Middle Ages. The ruling dynasty of medieval Padua had died out with Francesco Novello da Carrara whom the Venetians had murdered in 1405. The heiress Maria da Carrara was married to the Venetian patrician Niccolò Contarini less than a decade later. The site of the da Carrara castle at Piazzola was used for the construction of a Contarini villa in 1546, with a tenacious tradition ascribing the design to none other than Palladio himself. However, even the outlines of the sixteenth-century fabric eventually vanished beneath the elaborate embellishment of later generations and Palladio's putative role in the original project has never met with any acceptance.

The Contarini were one of the twelve so-called Apostolic families of Venice, present at the election of the first Doge in 697, but they made their most impressive dynastic contribution to Venice in the seventeenth century with a succession of no fewer than five doges. Nowhere is their splendour and power in this century more evident than at Piazzola where immensely long wings were added to the villa during the twenty-five years from 1659 to 1684, when Contarinis held office as the one-hundred-and-fourth and one-hundred-and-sixth doges of the Millenial Republic. These outbuildings made no pretense at being barchesse: they served to display Baroque architecture and ornamental motifs executed in stone outside, while inside an enfilade of endless rooms in each wing housed a library on the ground floor and a famous collection of paintings above. All this wealth, dispersed in rows, was abundantly obvious even from outside where there existed a basement of heavy rusticated half columns, worthy of Giulio Romano (1499 – 1546) at his most lavish, and an upper façade virtually crawling with caryatids whose heavily muscled torsos writhe under the weight of a heavy rooftop balustrade crowned with even more gesticulating stone statuary. This transformation of the barchessa wing into a rich and elongated architectural display became fashionable in the eighteenth century when several of the Brenta villas were extended by ornamental wings.

All of this provided the suitably splendid backdrop for one of the Veneto's most astonishing festivities, mounted in 1685 by the Contarini in honour of His Excellency and Serene Highness the Bishop of Osnabruck and Duke of Brunswick, Carousels of allegorical cars and festive carriages filled the forecourt; horses cavorted in the postures of the haute école; and mock naval battles were enacted on the fish pond. Inside, the ducal banquet excelled itself in extravagance, with endless tableaux vivants succeeding one another to a rich musical accompaniment from the four balconies that still overlook the great Sala della Chitarra (Guitar Room), so-called from its unusual shape. Following the rigid protocol of the day, the Duke sat in the center of a curved banquet table with fifteen guests, deemed grand enough to dine with him: only three women ranked sufficiently to join the party at table. In the center of the hall, an opening allowed the music to be heard below in the room appropriately known as the Sala delle Audizioni. Such was the fame of the entertainments at the villa during the seventeenth century that the Contarini installed a printing plant in one wing of the house to publish an account of their entertainments, such as that for the Duke of Brunswick, described in loving detail by Dottor Piccoli in his L'Orologio del Piacere, printed at Piazzola in 1685.

The small, two-storey, square pleasure pavilion known as the **Villa Emo-Capodilista** at Montecchia was designed by Dario Varotari (1534 – 96) for Gabriele Capodilista of Padua. The Capodilista were an ancient noble family whose command of a medieval regiment, distinguished by a coloured stripe or fascia, la lista, gave them their distinctive surname. The Capodilista had been invested with the fief of Montecchia since the fourteenth century, but by the time Gabriele brought Varotari there in the late sixteenth century, their principal residence was the Palazzo di San Daniele in Padua. The last of the family, Beatrice Capodilista, married the Venetian patrician Leonardo Emo in 1783, bringing her name to their many descendants, now divided into three branches represented in this selection by three exceptionally beautiful sixteenth-century villas: the Capodilista villa at Montecchia; the villa at Rivella, acquired from the Maldura, and the villa built by Palladio for the Emo at Fanzolo.

Documents in the family archives suggest that the parterre or platform on which the villa at Montecchia stands was rebuilt at about the time of the Emo-Capodilista alliance in the late eighteenth century. However, from its appearance there is every reason to believe that the design of this remarkable aspect of the villa's situation originated in the sixteenth century, and possibly with Varotari himself. A large square terrace, reflecting the shape of the building, was built up on the peak of the small Montecchia hill. A semicircular bastion was added to each side of this square and planted above as part of the villa's surrounding formal garden parterre. The curved stone wall was pierced from below by an arch and a ramp leading up to the villa from each of the four cardinal points of the compass. The ramp allowed the visitor to reach the house without dismounting while the arch served to introduce the theme of the extraordinary series of arcades that enclose the villa on all four façades.

The building at Montecchia was not intended as a residence, but as a pleasure pavilion to be reached from the Capodilista palace in Padua. During the recent postwar restoration of the villa and its wonderful fresco decoration an inscription was uncovered that recorded the performance there of a play first published in Venice in 1586, probably not long after the building had been completed. The villa provided a suitable backdrop for plays, festivities, banquets allegorical tableaux vivants and the court dancing, ancestor of le ballet, popular in late sixteenth-century Italy. The four rooms on each floor would have been hung with the richest silks for the occasion and hence Varotari decorated only the ceilings with fresco paintings of the gods and goddesses of antiquity. The most delightful of his inventions was the Sala della Pergola with a trompe l'œil balustrade around the base of the vault. Cherubs around the cornice play with dogs, parrots or a squirrel on a lead while grapevines heavy with clusters of fruit entwine their branches through a wooden pergola where still more putti climb and swing. Almost all of the other fresco subjects inside the building are taken from Ovid or from the legends of Rome while the vaults of the four loggias are tapestried with the popular grotesques copied from the recently excavated dining hall of Nero's Domus Aurea.

For all the pure simplicity of its interior and external symmetry and for the harmonious progression of its eight loggias and its remarkable staircase, it is the ornamental roof parapet that suggests Varotari's sense of the theatrical and acts as a harbinger of the Baroque taste to come in all the arts, but most obviously in architecture.

Casa di Petrarca (Petrarch's House), Arquà. The medieval village of Arquà grew up on a site that had been inhabited since prehistoric times in the Euganean Hills to the southwest of Padua. It was this remote rustic setting that provided the rich intellect and ceaselessly enquiring mind of the great poet Francesco Petrarca (1304 – 74) with a suitably rural retreat from the cares and distractions of the world. Petrarch first came to Arquà in 1369 as a guest of the Eremitani, monks of the Augustinian order who had early established a hermitage in the Euganean Hills. In the following year his friend and protector Francesco da Carrara, Lord of Padua, gave him a small property near the spring where the villagers drew their water. Four years later, on 19 July 1374, at dawn on the day before his seventieth birthday, the poet was found dead in the study of the small house he had built and loved at Arquà. Some versions of his life claim that a copy of Virgil's *Aeneid* lay open on his desk, while others claim it was *The Confessions of St. Augustine*. Thus his lifelong attempt to reconcile the virtues and values of pagan antiquity with his own devout Christianity confused the circumstances of his death as much as they enriched his own intellectual and aesthetic contribution to European literature and thought, earning him the posthumous reputation as "the first modern man."

By the time Petrarch had decided to build himself what he described as a "graziosa casetta circondata da un oliveto e da una vigna" (a delightful house surrounded by an olive grove and a vineyard), he had enjoyed many seasons of country life in a villa near Vaucluse in France. The area around the papal capital at Avignon had been his home from the age of seven until he was almost fifty years old. During this period he also travelled widely, being crowned Poet Laureate on the Capitoline Hill in 1341 and discovering the letters of Cicero in Verona in 1345. Not long before his death he gave the final form to his *Rerum vulgarum fragmenta*, better known as the *Canzoniere*, which earned him a fame more lasting than the Latin writing that was so admired in his own day. Save for one letter, no Italian prose of his survives while his Latin epistles, inspired by Cicero and composed at Arquà, sharpened his sense of an historical past until then unconceived of in European thought.

He wrote to his brother in 1373 of his life at Arquà, "... sebbene infermo nel corpo, io vivo nell'animo pienamente tranquillo, lungi dai tumulti, dai rumori,dalle cure, leggendo sempre e scrivendo e a Dio rendendo lodi e grazie..." (even though infirm, I live in the full tranquility of the spirit, far from upheavals, noise and cares: always reading, writing and rendering praise and thanksgiving to God...). Although his villa in the Euganean Hills was to be a hermitage and a retreat from the cares of the world, it was only a seasonal resort. He lived elsewhere in the winter and returned to Arquà in the heat of the summer. The large main hall with its original fourteenth-century wooden ceiling and the four adjacent rooms were the poet's principal apartment on the upper floor of the house, but the only original furniture to survive is a rustic folding chair and a desk. The large fireplaces in the main rooms as well as the handsome staircase and loggia were added to the house in the sixteenth century. Much of the original fresco decoration was redone in the seventeenth century. The poet's tomb, a simple sarcophagus of Verona marble, stands in the center of the village, erected in 1380 by the husband of his natural daughter Francesca.

A contemporary inscription records that the **Villa Emo** at Rivella was completed in 1588. The design for the building has been attributed to Vincenzo Scamozzi (1552 – 1616) and although recent research may cast doubts on these facts, no better documentation has emerged thus far. The villa was built on the Battaglia canal, an important waterway dug in 1189 to connect the River Bacchiglione and Vicenza with Este and other towns situated on the River Frassine, a tributary of the Adige. Several important villas were built on the canal in the sixteenth century, including one designed by Scamozzi for the Molin family only a short distance from Rivella. The house at Rivella was probably built for a branch of the Pernumia family on ancient feudal lands, but passed almost immediately to the Maldura from Padua. It came to the Emo-Capodilista in the late nineteenth century and has been beautifully and sensitively restored by the present generation of the family.

The house was probably not completed according to the original designs because only one *barchessa* was ever built whereas two were clearly intended. During the recent restoration, it was discovered that in the sixteenth century the villa had been prepared for fresco decoration that was never executed: perhaps the house never served as a principal residence for the Pernumia family. Architectural historians have also detected aesthetic discrepancies between the rich Corinthian colonnade and its tall base and the basic simplicity of the building's main block. This has led to the unsubstantiated supposition that the portico was added to the building at a later date. Nonetheless the Villa Emo at Rivella is undoubtedly one of the finest post-Palladian temple fronted villas built near Padua in the late sixteenth century.

The **Villa Barbarigo** at Valsanzibio was built sometime in the latter half of the seventeenth century in a sheltered position between two slopes of the Euganean Hills beneath Monte Ventolone. The villa itself belongs to a type frequently encountered in the Veneto. A plain stuccoed façade with a cluster of windows to mark the position of the *portego* hall on the *piano nobile* and, at the roof line, a raised central section crowned with a triangular pediment is surmounted by ornamental stone vases. The windows on the top floor are the largest openings in the façade, suggesting that the villa was designed to overlook a view or vista. And indeed, the rest of the Barbarigo's estate was planned with those vistas in mind. The fame of Val San Zibio, a local corruption of Sant' Eusebio, derives not from the villa, but from the great gardens, laid out in 1669 for Antonio Barbarigo who held the high office of Procurator in the Venetian government. His was one of the wealthiest and most prominent patrician families of the day and the gardens reflect the prestige of his clan in many of their details.

The garden is laid out along two axes. The longest runs up the slope of the hill immediately behind the house and is marked by a double row of tall cyprus trees. This axis is then continued from the terraces in front of the house to another, broader avenue, laid out in two lanes with a green verge between; this is bordered by one of the most spectacularly tall box hedges to be seen anywhere in Italy. The vista along this avenue continues as far as the eye can see until it meets the rise of the further slope and mounts again in the shape of another cypress-bordered path. However, before reaching this other slope, the main avenue encounters the second axis of the garden which crosses it at right angles. This is a much shorter section and drops down from the level of the avenue quite quickly to reach the marshy plain below. Clear channels that have now silted up once crossed this flat land and allowed the Barbarigo to reach their villa at Valsanzibio by boat. In fact, the immense gate at the foot of the garden's second axis served as the water entrance to the property. For all the simplicity of the villa's design, the water gate at Valsanzibio is one of the most elaborate examples of Baroque extravagance in the Veneto. A wide rectangular gate building is faced with six Ionic pilasters, separated by statuary niches with blind balustraded window openings above. Hunting trophies, sculpted in high relief, ornament the few remaining spaces of the façade while above the cornice, gigantic sections of broken curved pediment and balustrades support life-size hunting hounds. A great stone statue of Diana the Huntress crowns the whole from her vantage point on top of a tall belvedere. Behind the gate is a great fountain and another pond lined with grotto-like stone architecture. Steps rise to the garden's main avenue, with all the statuary turning to face Diana's Bath.

Much of the statuary here and elsewhere in the garden is identified by an enigmatic inscription, and the present owners have long sought the key to an allegorical programme with some esoteric significance. Having mounted the water terraces from the entrance gate dedicated to Diana, the visitor turns right and glimpses the villa at the end of the broad double path bordered by gigantic box hedges. Behind these hedges are the "garden rooms," each with a different theme, apparently in keeping with the secret meaning of the garden. There is a labyrinth, a statue of Time bearing a polyhedron and finally, the remarkable Rabbit Island where a great mound of earth for the animals' burrows was surrounded by a moat and crowned with an aviary that has since disappeared. However, much of this still appears exactly as detailed in the illustrated account of the gardens, *Le Fabbriche e Giardini della Casa Barbarigo*, published in Verona in 1702.

As visitors proceeded up the long avenue, stone benches invited them to rest, but the minute they sat down, the unsuspecting guests were doused by hundreds of hidden water-jets. Fleeing to the terrace gave no respite as the stone steps concealed yet more sprays, to the delight of the owner. Besides indulging in this typically eighteenth-century amusement, the Barbarigos were also obviously serious gardeners.

The **Villa dei Vescovi** at Luvigliano was built for the bishops of Padua as a retreat in the Euganean Hills. It was designed by the Veronese architect Giovanni Maria Falconetto (1468–1535) for Bishop Francesco Pisani and construction was probably begun in 1524. Building continued under various successive bishops for almost fifty years with the works being directed after 1561 by Andrea da Valle from Padua (active 1543–c.1577). Between 1567 and 1570 the forecourt was enclosed by a wall surmounted by ornamental scalloped battlements, constructed under another Bishop of the Pisani family; in 1579 Bishop Federico Cornaro was responsible for finishing the western side of the terrace with a staircase and a portico below. The villa itself, the earliest expression of classical Roman taste in Veneto villa architecture, was completed in 1567.

The single-storey arcading of the villa's principal façades and the massive simplicity of the great terrace on which it stands mask some of the building's complexity. As the road winds up the hills and through valleys to reach the villa, the three façades opened by the seven bays of a classical-style arcade are visible from every angle. Only the fourth, apparently unfinished, façade is hidden from the road. The villa is approached through a great triumphal arch, flanked by coupled Ionic columns, a reduced version of Vitruvius's first-century triumphal arch, *l'arco Gavi*, in Falconetto's native Verona. Once inside the forecourt, the massive scale of the villa's terrace becomes apparent and the way in which it served to raise the arcaded block in order to take advantage of the views.

The villa's single-storey arcade really rests on two basements. The first is formed by the gigantic brick-faced terrace that is so deep as to hide the second basement from view until the visitor has mounted the grandly balustraded staircases that rise in two flights to the upper level. From this level a two-branched staircase, rising in a single flight, leads to the arcading. This two-branched staircase is built against the wall of the true basement, or rather ground floor, of the villa. The ground floor appears quite low in relation to the magnificent arcades above. Its large plaster panels, scored to resemble rusticated stone, were already a standard part of the decorative repertory for a Renaissance building in 1524. From every angle, the Villa dei Vescovi is an architectural masterpiece. As the bishops and Falconetto must have intended, the eye immediately alights on the classical arcading, borrowed from Rome's Augustan Teatro di Marcello, and only subsequently takes in the rest of the structure on which it stands. Finally, photography reveals that the villa is not a single-storey arcaded structure, but an immense building fully three storeys high.

The final triumph of this wonderful villa is its colour. The deeply rich hues of brick are used for classical elements usually executed in stone, such as the pilasters, plinths, frames, capitals and even trigliphs which are highlighted here by a white stucco background. Stone is only used here as a leitmotif for the carved balustrades that surround each level and follow every diagonal rise of stairway. The overall impression is of brick red which, in its turn, complements the leafy green of the surrounding forested hills.

Villa Duodo, Monselice. A hilltop site for a villa in the Veneto suggests one of two things: either the owner wanted a pleasure pavilion or summer retreat like the Villa Capodilista or the Villa dei Vescovi near Padua, or like the Rotonda and the Rocca Pisana near Vicenza, or it meant that he was building on the foundations of an ancient castle. Monselice had been one of the most important fortified sites in the territory of medieval Padua. There was a large castle and a fortified village at the base of the hill as well as an upper redoubt. With the Venetian conquest of Paduan territory, first in the fifteenth century and then again after the treaty of Noyon in 1516, these strongholds were dismantled and the surrounding territories either auctioned off or assigned to Venetian families. The lower castle was given to the Marcello family while much of the surrounding territory, including the upper hill, fell to the extremely wealthy Duodo family.

In 1593 Pietro, son of the hero of Lepanto, Francesco Duodo, commissioned Vincenzo Scamozzi (1552–1616) to build a villa on the site of the old fortified redoubt, halfway up the hill beneath Frederick II's thirteenth-century fortress at the very summit. The steep site required heavily reinforced foundations and Scamozzi used "masegna" stone from the local trachite quarries for much of the building, an unusual material for Veneto villas. The house was a simple two-storey construction with a chapel built nearby, but the difficulty of erecting stone foundations for both these structures meant that work on the villa and its handsome domed chapel continued for almost twenty years. Access to the building was along a road that followed the line of the old fortifications up the hill and at the point where a great round bastion, La Rotonda, had stood, Scamozzi laid out a wide piazza with a Roman style triumphal arch opening on to the last straight road rising to the forecourt of the house. This arch recalls the similar device, attributed to Scamozzi's master Palladio, which opens on to the steep stairway leading to the famous hilltop shrine of Monte Berico at Vicenza. The chapel at Monselice, dedicated to St. George, must have seemed as important to the Duodo family as the Vicentine sanctuary, and they ordered Scamozzi to line the road to it with six devotional chapels. Before Pietro Duodo's death in 1611, the family had obtained for all of these chapels papal indulgences identical to those granted for visits to the seven basilicas of Rome, and Scamozzi's domed chapel next to the villa, inspired by Palladio's Tempietto di Maser, became a treasure house of important Christian relics. As the fame of these chapels increased so did the pride of the Duodo family and in 1740 Nicolò Duodo began an enlargement of the villa on plans by the Venetian architect Andrea Tirali (1660–1737) who had died only shortly before. In 1722 Tirali had been commissioned to design the new paving in stone in St. Mark's Square in Venice. He worked in stone at the Villa Duodo too and his new wing is one of the most successful additions to any Veneto villa, blending in perfectly with Scamozzi's more sober design of 150 years earlier. His façade has the central focus typical of Venetian and Veneto building, but the upper floor has three Venetian windows instead of one. In each case, the lateral bays are niches for statuary and the square openings above were also filled with sculptured panels. The rusticated stone frames surrounding the ground floor doors and windows echo Scamozzi's design, while opposite Scamozzi's wing Tirali planned a feature in the anals of villa construction in Italy. The entire hillside opposite the house was transformed into a broad staircase with a walled exedra at its summit. The long treads of the twenty-eight steps, rising through three landings, give the impression of an auditorium for a classical theater in which the villa's two façades below form the backdrop of an elaborate stage set almost as rich in sculpture and architecture as Palladio and Scamozzi's great joint masterpiece, the Teatro Olimpico in Vicenza.

The **Villa Giustinian** at Roncade lies at the very heart of Venice's earliest associations with the mainland. It is situated close to the Via Annia, an important commercial artery in the Roman Empire, which crossed the Tenth Region of Venetia-Histria. The villa is also near Altino, the ancient *Altinum*, one of the richest and most beautiful Roman cities in this part of Italy. Altinum was sacked and destroyed by Attila in 452 and again, by the Longobards, in 568. It was from this Roman town that the very first refugees from the barbarian invasions sought sanctuary in the Venetian lagoon. Their settlement in the islands was marked by a small tower, Il Torcello, from which they could see their abandoned homes at Altino. Roncade also enjoys access to the lagoon from a nearby tributary of the River Sile, which once flowed directly into the great delta surrounding Venice.

The very name Giustinian also recalls the most remote period of Venice's foundation. The ancient chronicles claimed that the Giustinian family originated with the great Justinian and his nephew and son-in-law, the Emperor Justin. Justin's son John came to Istria in 670 and founded Justinopolis, today known as Capodistria in Yugoslavia. From there his descendants emigrated to Venice where their coat-of-arms bore the two-headed eagle of the Byzantine Empire. The story of the family's near extinction in the twelfth century was one of the most popular in early Venetian history. All the Giustiniani men had perished in battle save for one, a monk called Nicolò, who lived at the Lido. So great had been the family's prestige that the government petitioned the Pope to release Nicolò from his vows so that he could marry Anna, daughter of Doge Vitale Michiel II. The union was a success resulting in a healthy progeny, after which Nicolò returned to his monastery and Anna retired to a convent she founded in the islands. One of the most noteworthy of their descendants was the first patriarch of Venice, St. Lorenzo Giustinian (1381–1456). By the end of the fifteenth century Girolamo Giustinian and his wife Agnesina of the ancient Badoer family had acquired the lands of the Sanzi family at Roncade and ordered a villa to be built there.

The Giustiniani house at Roncade was conceived of as a villa at the center of an important agricultural property and not as the castle its battlemented walls and defense towers suggest. Despite a lack of documentation, all the earliest references to the house make it clear that the Giustiniani ordered that their new villa be surrounded by these trappings of medieval fortification as a tribute to the feudal powers of their predecessors at Roncade, the ancient Sanzi family. Curious as their elaborate tribute may seem, there is evidence that ancient feudal traditions had a romantic appeal for fifteenth-century Venetian patricians whose own family traditions were, like those of the Giustiniani, of quite a different order.

The architecture of the villa at Roncade is fascinating, not only as a pastiche of fourteenth-century Veneto fortification, but also because the graceful double loggia designed for the façade is crowned by a classical triangular pediment: it therefore represents the sole surviving prototype for Palladio's double porticos at the Villa Cornaro at Piombino Dese and at the villa built by him on the outskirts of Montagnana for the Pisani family. But even without these subsequent derivations, the loggia at Roncade is important as a rare example in the Veneto of the graceful late fifteenth-century architecture associated in Venice with the descendants of Pietro Lombardo (1435–1515) and known as Lombardesque architecture.

The simple outlines and delicate late fifteenth-century architecture of the **Villa Corner Fiammetta** (formerly Villa dall'Aglio) on the River Sile represent a delightful interlude in the Venetian presence on the mainland between the conquest of the Veneto in the early fifteenth century and the terrible defeat of Venice in 1509 at the hands of the armies of the League of Cambrai. Much of the charm of this period, reflected in the exquisite outlines of the Villa Corner, is to be found in literary sources. And this literature can be associated, as can this particular villa, with the presence in the Veneto of an extraordinary historical personage, Queen Catherine Cornaro of Cyprus (1454–1510).

Catherine was a member of a Venetian family whose legendary riches derived from Cyprus where the island's rulers often found themselves indebted to the Cornaro. She was married in 1468 to the King of Cyprus, James II, and, from her widowhood six years later, she governed the island alone until 1489. The Venetian Republic then took over her realms in exchange for a tiny kingdom in the Veneto at Asolo and a rich annuity. Although her role as patroness of the arts has been somewhat discredited of late, there exists a famous portrait of her by Gentile Bellini in Budapest and she commissioned an unknown architect to build the Villa dall'Aglio as a wedding present for her maid of honour, Fiammetta.

But although the villa perpetuates the memory of one of Catherine's entourage, the story of this wonderful gift was recounted by another of her courtiers, the learned poet and man of letters Cardinal Pietro Bembo (1470–1547). Bembo refers to Fiammetta in his *Asolani*, Platonic dialogues on love, part narrative and part lyric poetry, written around 1497, published in 1507, and dedicated to the Duchess of Ferrara, the legendary Lucrezia Borgia. Bembo's choice of rural Asolo, clustered around Catherine's two castles, as a setting for his poetic and philosophical meditations on love, helped to foster the pastoral or bucolic mode in late fifteenth-century Italian literature. And in turn, this literary fashion, whether expressed in the vulgar tongue Bembo helped to perfect or in learned Latin imitations of classical authors, found a counterpart in the increasing prominence and importance given to pure landscape in Venetian painting, especially in the masterpieces of the great Veneto artist, Giorgione di Castelfranco (?1478–1510).

Just as an increased interest in the countryside influenced the literary and artistic conventions of an urban or courtly society, so the countryside borrowed its architecture from the city at this time. The Villa dall' Aglio could have come straight from Jacopo de' Barbari's woodcut aerial view of Venice dated 1500, which shows an almost identical building on the Giudecca island in the foreground. Since few of these late fifteenth-century palaces with a garden side-arcade survive in Venice (the Palazzo Bernardo on the Grand Canal in the parish of San Barnaba is virtually unique) the Villa dall 'Aglio is an important illustration of a building type familiar and even widespread in early Renaissance Venice. The compact block of the building, constructed of brick and stucco; the absence of projecting eaves; the capped spark trap chimneys; and the cluster of windows in the center of the façade at the *piano nobile*; even the closely laid beams in the loggia are all the unmistakable hallmarks of Venetian palace architecture and construction, recently and beautifully restored by the villa's present owners. The villa is a worthy representation of that prelude to Venice's great golden age that took place in the last few decades of the fifteenth century.

Villa Cornaro, Piombino Dese. This villa, designed by Palladio in 1553 for the Venetian patrician Giorgio Cornaro, eventually served as the prototype for many of the southern plantation houses built in eighteenth-century America. Palladio himself used the Villa Cornaro's distinctive double portico motif on only one other country house. A later generation of Veneto architects did reproduce it, although much less often and with less success than the more usual Palladian classical temple front portico. In Palladio's own day, the size, shape, decoration and even the porticos of each villa would have been determined by criteria of decorum largely lost to us today. Clearly neither of his double portico houses was intended as a farm villa in the traditional sense. Villa Pisani stands on the edge of the village of Montagnana and Palladio's own description of the Villa Cornaro makes it evident that this building was also designed to reflect its somewhat suburban location. In both cases, these houses contain important apartments on the ground floor as well as full reception rooms above. The upper loggia was undoubtedly designed to overlook the garden parterres which were an integral part of these suburban properties. In this they most closely resembled those villas built in the islands of the Venetian lagoon as pleasure retreats for the local patriciate. However, the idea of crowning the double portico with a triangular pediment was probably inspired by that feature of the Villa Giustinian at Roncade, at that time considered one of the Veneto's most important examples of late fifteenth-century architecture.

The portico at the front of the Villa Cornaro projects far forward, as does its prototype at Roncade, while the matching motif on the garden front was recessed into the square outlines of the building. Twin stairways, each as broad as the portico's six-columned width, provide a base for a composition executed according to classical decorum, with the Ionic order on the lower floor and the richer Corinthian capitals reserved for the upper loggia. The main hall of the Villa Corner is a 32-foot square with four Ionic columns set out to support the hall above. Yet the principal ornament of this impressive reception room are six niches set curiously close to the corners of the room. The width of these niches corresponds to the space between the four columns and the wall, but otherwise represents an awkward arrangement.

In the niches stand life-size statues of members of the Cornaro family, designed by the Vicentine sculptor Camillo Mariani (1567–1611). They were executed in plaster between 1587 and 1597, well after the death of both Palladio and his patron at Piombino Dese, Giorgio Cornaro. In fact, it appears that the upper loggia was not completed until this time. Whatever the reasons for these delays, the Corner were one of the richest and most prominent families of the Venetian patriciate. Giorgio's father had been a patron of Sansovino and had commissioned the great Palazzo Corner della Ca' Grande on the Grand Canal, while Giorgio's heirs saw to it that the members of the family commemorated in plasterwork statuary would enjoy the company of their most illustrious forebears, Queen Catherine Cornaro of Asolo and her husband, the King of Cyprus.

The **Villa Marcello** at Levada is the finest, most elegant example of a farm villa to survive with its eighteenth-century decoration and furnishing intact in the Veneto. The Marcello, one of the very few families in Italy with an unimpeachable claim to direct descent from a Roman *gens*, have worked the land at Levada since the sixteenth century. The central block of villa and the twin arcaded *barchesse* date from that period, but the magnificent Palladian appearance of the façade and the splendid interior decoration of the house belong to Venice's second golden age and also to a slightly different ramification of their widespread family tree. In the eighteenth century an heiress of the Levada branch married into the Maruzzi family, Balkan bankers from Epirus whose cosmopolitan connections made them the Rothschilds of eighteenth-century eastern Europe. It was their wealth that completely transformed the villa at Levada into the magnificent country seat of the Marcello today. The Maruzzi's daughter married into a Russian family – an unsurprising move, since by that time the Maruzzi were using part of their great wealth to subsidize the debts of the Empress of Russia, Catherine the Great. However, the Russian Lord of Levada cared so little for his villa in the Veneto that he lost the entire estate on the turn of a card. At this point, the Marcello from the neighbouring estate at Badoer offered to buy it from his lucky adversary, who cared even less for the villa. Levada was therefore returned to its original owners who have resided there ever since, showing exemplary care over its preservation.

But in spite of the care with which the Villa Marcello at Levada has been maintained, little or nothing is known for certain about the circumstances of its origin, because the family archives were destroyed in a fire that devastated Badoer in 1920. Obviously the sixteenth-century block had been enlarged and embellished by the Maruzzi around 1750 and although the name of the architect remains a mystery, the similarity to the Villa Pisani at Stra, begun in 1735 by Francesco Maria Preti (1701–74), is quite marked. At Levada the tall ground floor façade, punctuated with six windows and the front door, is decorated with a motif of rustication similar to that at Stra, while on the *piano nobile* the half columns stretch up through an attic floor as well, giving the ballroom on this floor space for a handsome gallery arranged very like that at the Villa Pisani.

Whereas the Pisani had used Tiepolo to depict their glory in fresco at Stra, the glory of the Maruzzi was of a different order and Tiepolo had since left the Veneto for the court of Madrid, never to return. The Maruzzi resorted to Giovanni Battista Crosato (1697–1756) to paint the full splendour of Olympus on their ballroom ceiling. By this time Crosato's credentials were almost as impressive as Tiepolo's and the frescoes at Levada, including the large panels with scenes from the life of Alexander the Great, were executed at the end of a long career culminating in his fresco decoration of the Palazzina di Caccia at Stupinigi for the King of Sardinia. In addition to these frescoes, the villa is renowned for the quality and variety of its stuccowork decoration: from the most magnificently exuberant framing for Crosato's painting to the charming gilded ribbons and plasterwork frames for mirror-backed candle sconces; or ever more elaborate set pieces, holding large mirrors above the fireplaces, or the amusingly naive scenes of peasant life, worked in bedroom walls by an anonymous itinerant stuccador. All of this ornament and decoration finds a perfect complement in the fine suites of *mobili di villeggiatura* (country villa furniture) crafted in the eighteenth century by the estate carpenter and still maintained in place by the present generation of the Marcellos at Levada.

The **Villa Rinaldi**, situated in the hills just below Asolo, is generally considered one of grandest country houses in the province of Treviso. However, from the road that passes in front of it, as with many other villas in the Veneto, the full splendour of the edifice is not immediately apparent. The small roadside family chapel is built in a fine Baroque style with a remarkably tall bell-tower. But bell-towers in the Veneto, whether of family chapels or parish churches, often reached great heights, ringing out the hours of the day across the surrounding flat farmlands. The grandeur of the Villa Rinaldi reveals itself only gradually, first in its commanding position on a rise overlooking the surrounding land and then in the broad staircase leading up to the terrace on which the villa was built. Either side of this approach is lined with large outbuildings. The tall façade of the villa itself is crowned with seven statuary figures standing on the roof, and is also flanked by wings enlivened by a particularly graceful double range of fresco-decorated loggias. These loggias and the façade are the first real indication of the marvels contained in the house. In fact, the original two-storey villa had been built in a rather restrained style in the early seventeenth century and then, in 1663, Francesco Rinaldi (1621–98) ordered the façade to be raised by another floor. It was he who commissioned the construction of the arcaded wings and the artistic embellishment of the whole: not only the rooftop statuary and the stone coat-of-arms with its attendant elephants, but also those pieces placed on the gate posts and balustrades, or executed in high relief stucco for the chimney hoods of the great red Verona marble fireplaces. In describing all that Francesco Rinaldi ordered for his "palazzo a Asolo", an anonymous eighteenth-century author enthusiastically compared the artistic treasures of Villa Rinaldi with those of Prince Borghese in Rome. However exaggerated such a comparison now seems, there is no question that the fresco decoration of the villa by Pietro Liberi (1614–87) and the younger Venetian Andrea Celesti (1637–1712) is quite spectacular by any standards. Liberi avoided architectural elements in his frescoed rooms, preferring to envelop the family in all-embracing landscapes peopled by nymphs and satyrs, or with cloudy heavens supporting the entire cast of Olympus. Several of the themes appear to have been borrowed from Veronese's masterpieces for the nearby Villa Barbaro at Maser, while one room is dedicated to the Battle of the Giants, taken almost directly from Giulio Romano's inspired invention of this kind of fresco work at the Palazzo del Te near Mantua.

Celesti's fresco work in the villa was executed between 1705 and 1707 and in it is evident the calmer, less turbulent taste of neo-Classicism, or in this case, neo-Palladianism. *Trompe l'œil* architecture is once again an important element in framing scenes of pure landscape, as it had been for Veronese at Maser, while on the ground floor the fine staircase to the *piano nobile* is recreated in *trompe l'œil* fresco on an opposite wall. Virtually every surface of the interior, including the underside of the stairs, is covered in painted decoration, although some of the finest work was executed in simple old-fashioned patterns used to ornament the beamed ceilings in the secondary rooms of the house.

The great **Villa Barbaro** at Maser, built by Andrea Palladio (1508–80) during the 1550s for the brothers Marc'Antonio and Daniele Barbaro, is undoubtedly the best known and most admired of all the country houses in the Veneto after La Rotonda. Palladio's wonderfully warm yellow façade, picked out with white classical detail and set against the dark green background of the hillside, is without doubt a visual and aesthetic success of the highest order, but the villa also owes its extraordinary fame to the fresco decoration of the interior by Paolo Veronese (1528–88). Italy's greatest works in fresco painting are usually associated with Tuscan artists, from Giotto through the generations of the Florentine Renaissance – Massaccio, Frà Angelico, Andrea Castagno, Frà Filippo Lippi, Benozzo Gozzoli and many others – to works in the Tuscan tradition such as those of Leonardo da Vinci in Milan or Michelangelo and Raphael in Rome. Veronese's frescoes at Maser also deserve to be ranked with these masterworks of painting: the Maser cycle includes figures from the classical pantheon, as well as allegorical figures of both obvious and less apparent significance. The artist also depicted real people such as Giustiniana Giustinian, Marc'Antonio Barbaro's wife: she is accompanied by an old wet-nurse who seems to point a finger at the visitors below, irrespective of their position in the room.

Another contemporary figure, dressed for hunting, appears at a doorway at the end of a long enfilade and is so striking as to be identified with Veronese himself, while in another room the artist has depicted one of the Barbaro's pet spaniels or painted his own brushes and slippers left lying on a *trompe l'œil* dado. The flat walls of the interior are ornamented with mouldings, brackets, frames, cornices and even fluted columns and Corinthian capitals, perfectly counterfeited in all their tangible three dimensional reality, while other stretches of coloured plaster open out on to sunny vistas of distant landscapes or scenes of villa life. These scenes, which blend so naturally with the rural setting of the house, were the very first excursion into pure landscape painting in the history of European art.

Because of the Barbaro brothers' patronage, much of the subject matter of the fresco programme at Maser was determined by them, and although the overall meaning remains obscure, the most important part of the cycle in the Sala dell'Olimpo is usually interpreted as referring to the horoscope of one or both of the brothers. The strange statuary of the Nymphaeum was designed by Alessandro Vittoria (1524–1608) to illustrate a programme conceived by Marc'Antonio. One of the most prominent patrician servants of the Serenissima, Marc'Antonio Barbaro had been sent as Venetian ambassador to the court of Catherine de' Medici at the height of the wars of religion and had been the representative or *bailo* at Constantinople on the eve of the Battle of Lepanto. The Republic rewarded him with the rank of Procurator for life, the second highest dignity in the state. His brother Daniele (1513–70), was no less prominent a figure within the Church. He had held office at the Republic's great university of Padua and had been an ambassador to England during the difficult years following the death of Henry VIII. In 1550 he was nominated by the Venetian state to the great ecclesiastical benefice of Aquileia. As Patriarch-elect he eventually attended the Council of Trent, but was also able to pursue those intellectual and antiquarian interests typical of the sixteenth-century clergy. In 1556 he edited and commented a new edition of Vitruvius's *De architectura* in translation. The triumphant careers of the Barbaro brothers seem enshrined in their rich and magnificent country house, a highly original blend of Veneto farm villa architecture with the kind of urban sophistication characteristic of the terra firma's more aggressively classical pleasure pavilions. At Maser their ancient coat-of-arms, a red circlet on a white ground, representing the blood stain made on a white napkin by the severed head of a Saracen, is flanked by two of Vittoria's finest reliefs: nude supporters with both a double headed Imperial eagle and the triple tiara of the papacy alluding to the twin poles of their worldly accomplishments.

Almost as impressive as Palladio's magnificent design for the **Villa Emo** at Fanzolo di Vedelago is the fact that, over four hundred years later, it is still owned by the family for whom it was built and that the present generation still farms the surrounding lands, as they did centuries ago. The Emo family had long been prominent members of the Venetian patriciate when Leonardo Emo acquired enormous estates in the plains near Castelfranco in the first half of the sixteenth century. For the many reasons already discussed in the introduction, the Venetian Republic was at that time encouraging the patriciate to invest its capital in estates on the mainland and to supervise personally the reclamation and cultivation of the land. The Emos who commissioned Palladio to build his great masterpiece for them at Fanzolo became so thoroughly identified with the mainland that the origins of their power and prosperity in Venice and their former maritime fortunes were virtually eclipsed and almost forgotten. Only the figure of the last great captain general of the Venetian navy, Admiral Angelo Emo, revived the memory of the Emo's former greatness in the service of the city and its fleet. The Emo-Capodilista family, one branch of which lives at Fanzolo, is still one of the most prominent in the Veneto, but none of its many members lives in Venice and the sundry family palaces on the Grand Canal are today known by other names.

In spite of the continued presence of the Emos at Fanzolo and the critical studies that have been made of Palladio's masterpiece, little is known for certain about the chronology of the building's conception or the phases of its construction. The Villa Emo is generally assumed to have been built around 1560 with the wonderful fresco decoration of the interior completed by Giambattista Zelotti (1526–78) in 1563. This fresco cycle, which has survived in a remarkable state of preservation, is undoubtedly Zelotti's masterpiece. Its themes are an illustration of many cross currents of mid sixteenth-century artistic taste. The life-size figures of chained male nudes, usually identified as prisoners, owe a great deal to Michelangelo's *Ignudi* in the Sistine Chapel and also to his statuary for the Medici family tombs at San Lorenzo in Florence. The trophies of arms and banners allude to recent Venetian victories over the armies of Cambrai on the mainland and over the Turks at sea. Indeed one of the villa's most precious historical relics is the coat-of-arms retrieved from a Venetian war galley commanded by a member of the Emo family. The *trompe l'œil* architecture in all the main reception rooms is emphatically classical in detail, as are the Roman busts, also executed in fresco work.

The most striking feature of the villa's decorations are the large frescoed scenes taken from classical mythology or from the legends of ancient Rome. Many of them seem to illustrate a moral about marital fidelity – cycles depicting the story of Virginia, the love of Venus and Adonis, the marriage of Hercules or Jupiter and Io – although the ultimate significance of the overall programme has thus far defied analysis. The handsome single figures, representing the Arts or the Four Seasons, are easier to interpret, although their juxtaposition with religious subjects such as The Holy Family, the Noli Me Tangere or the Penitence of St. Jerome seem to hint at an approach to Christian and pagan allegory that eludes interpretation today. For all the spectacular effect and colour of this painted decoration, the rooms of the Villa Emo still seem perfectly proportioned architectural units quite in keeping with the simplicity of the building's *barchesse* and its recessed temple front façade, constructed with the most severe of the classical orders, the Doric. Only the triangular pediment serves to suggest a more pompous note with the splendidly carved winged victories, attributed to Alessandro Vittoria (1524–1608), supporting the Emo coat-of-arms.

The **Rocca Pisana** at Lonigo was built according to a design of Palladio's disciple and collaborator Vincenzo Scamozzi (1552–1616). It was intended as a summer retreat in the hills near Lonigo for Vittor Pisani, a member of the great Venetian patrician family who were also feudal Counts of Bagnolo on the mainland. The administrative center of their fief was located in the villa Palladio had built for them at Bagnolo in 1544 while their principal residence, an enormous palace in Lonigo, was begun in 1557. Scamozzi's project for the Rocca is thought to have been submitted in 1576 and the building completed by 1578. Of all the great building projects planned for the Pisani in the neighbourhood of Lonigo, the Rocca Pisana is the only one that seems to have been completed according to the plans for it.

Scamozzi's debt, to Palladio in general and to La Rotonda in particular, is immediately obvious, yet the success of the Rocca is of a different order from that of its great Palladian prototype. The Rotonda's four great temple porticos are its most extraordinary feature, unanticipated even in classical antiquity, while it is the Rocca's interior, and especially its domed hall that is Scamozzi's greatest achievement. However, the Rocca Pisana was a unique tour de force in Scamozzi's career while Palladio created one masterpiece after another. For all the restrained harmony of the Rocca's exterior and for all the purity of the domed hall at the heart of the building, Scamozzi's plan, as published in his *L'Idea dell' Architettura Universale* (Venice 1615), lacks those harmonious interior proportions that are characteristic of Palladio's greatest conceptions. The original intention of both the Rocca and the Rotonda was otherwise virtually identical, with a perfectly circular central hall covered by a dome open to the elements, like that of the Pantheon in Rome. The dome of the Rocca is still open while the Rotonda's subsequent transformation from a pleasure pavilion into a farm villa rendered this feature of the building impracticable. Both their central halls are approached by four tall barrel-vaulted passages. At the Rotonda these lead out to the four porticos, while at the Rocca Scamozzi has designed large Serlian arcades open to the countryside on three sides and the front portico recessed within the main entrance façade on the fourth side.

But it is particularly in the decoration of the villa that Scamozzi's talents have found their finest expression. The exterior reflects the architect's preference for a kind of academic purity that anticipates the neo-Classical taste of eighteenth-century and early nineteenth-century Europe. The decoration of the domed hall is similarly stark, although additional elements of an extreme sophistication lend variety to its simple architecture. Four great niches rise almost to the cornice of the dome. Each niche contains a simply framed doorway leading to one of the four living rooms of the house and above each of these doors is a large rectangular window which serves to light the attic storey from the hall. The four walls between the great niches are flat and pierced by a much taller classical doorway which serves to frame the Serlian opening at the end of the corridor. Above these great doors, the attic is lit by a large oval aperture. Part of the beauty of this decoration lies in the simplicity of the framing elements, rendered in a glowing honey-coloured stone that contrasts with the cold white walls. It is in the dome itself that Scamozzi displays that architectural sophistication and artifice usually associated with the taste in the arts known as Mannerism. The cornice that might be expected to support the dome is present, but broken into eight heavy bracket-like sections from which broad bands or contrasting stone ribs rise to join the dome's hub, open to the sky. The dome, the very *raison d'etre* of the entire house, is thus laden with an ornamental embellishment lacking in every other part of the building. In fact, for the purity of its form and the light that issues from it, this domed interior is one of the finest creations of villa architecture of Venice's great golden age and a worthy model for the many country houses that subsequently derived from it.

The villa **La Rotonda** was designed by Andrea Palladio (1508–80) for a hilltop site just outside Vicenza. From every direction and vantage point, its domed center and four equal temple front porticos make a spectacular climax to the hilly rise on which it is situated. From inside the building its porticos open out on to uninterrupted views at all four points of the compass and it was for these views and for the cool breezes of this eminence that the villa was built. The architecture that Palladio created to exploit these elements proved one of his greatest inventions and the perfect representation of his genius; however, much of the building's design was obviously determined by his patron's requirements. In fact, Palladio devoted the first part of his description of the villa in the *Quattro Libri* to an account of Paolo Almerico's impressive credentials as a high official of the papal court. In this, Canon Almerico represented those twin poles of Roman influence in the taste of his times. As a man of the church, he represented the Rome of the papacy which, with its own recent history of humanistic culture under the great Della Rovere and Medici popes, had taken to cultivating, collecting and recreating the arts and architecture of Imperial Rome. The suburban villas built by the popes outside Rome in imitation of classical antiquity would be the inspiration for Canon Almerico's Rotonda on a hilltop outside his native Vicenza. Recent research indicates that Almerico had decided to come to Vicenza to prepare for his retirement sometime after the death of his mother in 1565. Although subsequent documentation in this case is fraught with contradictions, it would appear that he was able to make use of the building – whether still under construction or completed is unclear – by 1569 and he makes specific mention of it in a codicil added to his will in 1571. The way in which Canon Almerico used the building and the extent to which his requirements determined many of the most striking features of Palladio's architecture have been discussed in the introduction. On his death, the property passed to his natural son, who seems to have had little use for a pleasure pavilion in the suburbs. It was sold by him to the Capra family who over several successive generations saw to its continued embellishment on a lavish scale. It was they who were probably responsible for the ornamentation of the dome, with frescoes by Alessandro Maganza (1556–1630/40) and the richly heavy plasterwork statuary by Agostino and Virgilio Rubini, both active in the last decade of the sixteenth century. Even a hundred years later elaborate plasterwork was designed for the immense fireplaces in the villa and Lodovico Dorigny (1654–1742) was employed to fresco the lower walls of the circular central hall with a company of the principal gods and goddesses of the classical pantheon. The Capras showed no modesty with regard to their role in the embellishment of La Rotonda and proudly placed a Latin inscription on the principal portico proclaiming their ownership of the villa.

The Capra family were fully justified in their pride, having endowed the house with vast agricultural estates and commissioned Vincenzo Scamozzi (1552–1616) to transform Canon Almerico's pleasure pavilion into a farm villa. This Scamozzi accomplished with the construction of one of the most fascinating and little appreciated farm buildings in the history of architecture in the Veneto. On one side of the driveway up the slope to La Rotonda, he cut away part of the hill and built an enormously long *barchessa*. Approaching the villa up the drive, Scamozzi's *barchessa* is cleverly disguised as a low stone wall surmounted by a parade of ornamental statuary. A matching ornamental wall opposite serves to complete the illusion. However, a small door leads through the right-hand wall directly into the upper floor or granary of the *barchessa*. Below, the traditional arcading of a *barchessa* was rendered in giant rusticated square section piers, opening on to the farmyard. The *barchessa* could also be reached from the house by way of an extraordinary vaulted tunnel excavated through the hill. In fact, the subterranean architecture – kitchens, storerooms and vast freshwater cisterns extending under the drive – is no less fascinating than the extraordinary villa itself.

It is by marriage and inheritance, albeit through the female line, that the **Villa Pisani** at Bagnolo and La Rocca Pisana still belong to descendants of the great patrician family that built them over four hundred years ago. The very way in which the great estates near Lonigo came to the Pisani is equally representative of the history of the Republic in the Veneto. First, Lonigo itself, which had been an important and frequently contested feudal terrritory in the Middle Ages, submitted voluntarily to Venice during the Republic's conquest of a mainland empire in the early fifteenth century. However, during the onslaught of the League of Cambrai, the local lords of the Nogarola family sided with the forces of the Empire and after the treaty of Noyon had their properties confiscated as punishment for their betrayal of Venice. The Pisani acquired the Nogarola castle and its surrounding lands and were also invested with feudal rights over a vast area.

In the early 1540s, in compliance with Venetian dispositions, the Pisani employed Andrea Palladio to convert the Nogarola castle into a villa. Thanks to the efforts of his patron and protector, the learned Giangiorgio Trissino (1478–1550), Palladio was becoming increasingly well-known in Vicentine circles but the Pisani were the first of the great patrician families of Venice to employ him. His brief at Bagnolo was a special one, as can be seen to this day. The stonework visible in the foundations and even in the towers at Bagnolo indicate that Palladio reused elements from the original Nogarola castle. This unusual circumstance also helps to explain some of the villa's interior proportions. The main hall is fully twice as wide as the side rooms, while its height includes one and a half times this great breadth. Such an area is vastly out of proportion in terms of Palladio's subsequent projects for farm villas in the Veneto and is best explained by assuming that Palladio was directed by the Pisani simply to cover over and vault the castle's former courtyard space. While such a provision and the resulting size of the great hall hardly seem appropriate to a villa, it is important to bear in mind that the Pisani used Bagnolo as the administrative center of their feudal holdings, with the villa's hall serving as the public tribunal for their administration of the Republic's justice. As already mentioned, they soon commissioned a huge palace in Lonigo itself as their country residence. The scale of their project for outbuildings at Bagnolo – surrounding an area the size of St. Mark's Square in Venice – again reinforced the impression that the Pisani intended Bagnolo to be a huge entrepot for their vast agricultural holdings and not just a family farm villa.

Recent research supports the idea that the Villa Pisani was complete by 1544, only a few years after Palladio's return from his first visit to Rome. His Roman studies with Trissino are reflected in the great lunette window that lights the central hall at Bagnolo and that owes its form to the kind of window Palladio observed and copied in the Baths of Diocletian. The ruins of that great classical building also inspired his interest in the varying elevation of a building's interior. The article he wrote in the *Quattro Libri* describing the Villa Pisani dwells on this concern. Palladio's published woodcut plan of the villa shows a classical portico that was probably never realized and today it is the loggia facing the River Gua that survives as the villa's principal façade. The arches framed in rusticated stone can be traced to classical prototypes such as the vomitoria arches in a Roman arena or in the Colosseum, while the great triangular pediment above this loggia masks a huge granary located on the upper floor of the house. The recent renovation of the villa has successfully restored the harmonious beauty that Palladio alone knew how to bestow on an essentially simple structure – in this case the remodelled castle of the disgraced Nogarola lords of Bagnolo.

The **Villa Pojana** was designed by Andrea Palladio (1508–80) for Bonifacio Pojana, member of an ancient family whose proudest traditions, like those of many mainland aristocrats, were of a military nature, their service as mercenary commanders or *condottiere* offered to whomever seemed the dominant power of the day. By Palladio's time, the Veneto had returned to the relatively peaceful sway of the Venetian Republic and many of these erstwhile warriors turned from war-like pursuits to agriculture. Palladio's project for the Villa Pojana appears to have dated from around 1550, since the building as we know it was still not complete by 1555 and the fresco decoration was added only in 1563. However, beyond these dates, little else concerning this curious building is accurately documented.

The most puzzling aspects of the villa are the discrepancies that exist between the present building and the plan for it published in Palladio's *Quattro Libri*. But such inconsistencies are not unique to the Villa Pojana and their importance should not be exaggerated. The villa's external appearance has always been the subject of great critical comment and speculation while it must have been the interior of the house that concerned the owner most of all. The interior is as fine an example as any of Palladio's sense of proportion and harmony. The symmetry of the layout derives from the conventions of Veneto villa construction and, in turn, from their ultimate source in Venice's palace architecture. However, Palladio's abiding interest, inspired by his study of the Roman baths, with a sequence of varied elevations inside the building, is well illustrated in the Villa Pojana. To achieve the desired result, Palladio simply inserted an upper floor above one or more of the side rooms, leaving the central hall, ultimately corresponding to the Venetian palace's *sala del portego*, taller than the other rooms in the villa. However, there were certain refinements in this arrangement at Pojana. Although not apparent from outside the villa, this upper floor crosses the building above the loggia, effectively enclosing the greater height of the central hall on three sides. The *portego* at Pojana is a magnificent space, but the side rooms, with their rich fresco decoration by Bernardino India (c.1528–90) and another artist from Verona, Anselmo Canera (active between 1566 and 1575), are among the most handsomely proportioned of the Palladian repertoire. Two small staircases were fitted in between these rooms and the central hall. They descend to the ground floor where Palladio had planned the kitchens and storerooms and they also reach the attic which, in the case of the Villa Pojana, was used from the outset as a granary.

The extensive outbuildings or *barchesse* foreseen in the original plan were never constructed and only one of the wings that Palladio designed was ever built, and then only in the eighteenth century by Francesco Muttoni. Even though incomplete, the Villa Pojana is distinguished by one of Palladio's most remarkable, if seldom imitated, decorative motifs. This is the Serlian opening to the entrance loggia where the central arch is surrounded by a framing motif pierced by five blind round openings. This curious device has caused endless speculation, especially since it does not appear in Palladio's woodcut illustration of the villa in the *Quattro Libri*. It may have derived from an unrealized idea of Bramante's or even from that architect's use of a similar design over the triumphal arch in Santa Maria delle Grazie in Milan. Palladio and Bonificio Pojana may have even intended it to have some esoteric significance linked with a programme to be carried out in the direction of the villa and its garden. But until it has been satisfactorily explained, it remains one of the most original and distinctive ornamental motifs in the entire repertoire of Palladian architecture and the identifying signature of the Villa Pojana.

The villa on the River Bacchiglione at Montegaldella near Vicenza, known as **"La Deliziosa,"** was built in 1622 for the Conti family and passed to the Lampertico family about 250 years later. In 1741 the gardens and park next to the house were enclosed by a wall whose entrances today display the finest series of exquisite wrought-iron gates to be found anywhere in the Veneto, if not in all Italy. Each composition is a delightful example of the craftsman's fantasy while the quality of the workmanship is so high that scholars, such as Professor Renato Cevese, who suggests they are the work of Maestro Zuanne Baccio Albertale, have long sought to identify the artist. The area behind these gates was laid out as a *parc à l'anglaise* by the Lampertico family. Unfortunately only the fine garden statues by the Marinali workshops now survive to suggest the architecturally richer formal parterres that must have once existed around the villa.

The villa itself was "remodernized" in 1868, although the documents in which this operation is recorded are unclear with regard to the architect. The end result is not unpleasing, but presents a number of puzzling inconsistencies for the student of Veneto villa architecture. Fortunately these have been resolved by the recent publication of a plan of the property, still in the Lampertico archives, which presents an obviously authentic record of the villa's seventeenth-century appearance.

Originally the villa's portico was intended to be open across its entire wide front with five, and not three, free-standing giant Ionic columns. The attic storey above was then only three bays wide, crowned with a conventional triangular pediment. Statues stood at its three corners, while two remaining stone figures were placed on plinths at the outer edges of the façade. A sloping wall linked this end of the façade with the corner of the pediment to accentuate the tall vertical orientation of the design. Today the magnificent colonnade is the dominant feature, giving the villa's appearance a heavy horizontal thrust. The "remodernization" resulted in more living space, with the extra rooms on either end of the attic storey and the two extensions to the mezzanine projecting between the outer columns of the façade.

The Lampertico family needed all the room they could get because, despite the magnificence of the façade, the building behind it is smaller than might be expected. The ground floor has only three rooms, none of which is as deep as the portico. The central room opens out into what remains of the Conti's elaborately ornamented garden where the principal survival is *La Macchina*, a popular word for fantastic compositions in statuary that might be rendered in English as "The Contrivance." La Macchina at Montegaldella was designed or contrived by Orazio Marinali (1643–1720) to symbolize the four parts of the world. An elaborate base surrounded by minor plinths supports lolling statues in the attitudes of Roman river gods, while allegorical figures stand around the central pier which serves as a pedestal for Jove and his attendant eagle. Marinali and his family workshop supplied "La Deliziosa" with 164 other statues well after the founder's death. This is the famous series of figures carved in the lively, indeed exaggerated, attitudes of characters from the Commedia dell'Arte tradition: Venice's Pantalone, Bologna's Doctor Graziano and Arlecchino from Bergamo, where the most famous itinerant companies originated, and even farther afield with Pulcinella from Naples. Many of the characters and indeed the conventions of these improvised comedies may have originated in the Veneto in the late sixteenth century, but it was in the eighteenth century that their frivolous appearance and characteristic attitudes, sometimes verging on the acrobatic, became part of the European artistic convention. Marinali's garden statuary at Montegaldella is a masterpiece of the genre, equal in its way to the porcelain figurines created by Kaendler or Bustelli, to the exquisite engravings of Stefano della Bella or to Watteau's melancholy portrait of the French actor Gilles, in the costume of Pierrot.

The **Villa-castle Grimani Marcello** at Montegalda is the one building in this selection of Veneto villas – and one of the very few to survive in the ancient territories of the Venetian Republic – that can trace its origins to an important complex of medieval fortification. As has been mentioned before, it was the deliberate policy of the Republic after the conquest of the mainland in the early fifteenth century to see to the dismantling of fortification in its newly acquired territories, or else, in the case of feudal estates and castles, to assign them to Venetian or mainland families of an unimpeachable loyalty. The castle of Montegalda was Venice's gift in 1455 to the Vicentine nobleman Chierichino Chiericati. The Chiericati family held it for precisely one hundred years and then sold it to a member of Venice's patriciate, Andrea Contarini. From then on it passed from one Venetian patrician family to another until the present owner purchased it from the Grimani Marcello. Major alterations to its structure were made in the seventeenth century and again between 1750 and 1770; an extensive cycle of fresco decoration was begun in 1780 by Andrea Urbani and completed two years later.

But it is naturally the medieval structures, or what remains of them as documented in the few scattered references and archives, that conjure up a picture of the castle's history. Today a great mass of masonry rises from a site on top of Montegalda, a hill located almost mid-way between Vicenza's Monte Berico and the Euganean Hills southeast of Padua. The ancient outer perimeter is almost circular, while low structures inside the walls were built up later to make a rectangular courtyard. Four towers rise above the castle walls, but the determination of subsequent generations to transform the building from a fortress into a residence or villa eliminated all evidence of the defensive function of these towers. Only the tall drawbridge tower seems redolent of siege, warfare and surprise sorties. And today the ancient portcullis opens on to an elegantly balustraded bridge, decorated with eighteenth-century statuary leading down a flight of steps to a beautiful parterre planted in the most sophisticated traditions of the Italian formal garden.

Inside the courtyard, one of these towers rises up above the perimeter walls and swallow-tail merlons are visible beyond the rooftops. Such battlements as these are often associated with the Veneto's greatest castle-builders, the Della Scala of Verona and documents recount Cangrande Della Scala's capture of the fortress on two occasions: in 1312 when he put it to the flame and again, in 1314, when he took it from the Paduans. His canting coat-of-arms, blazoned with a ladder or *scala*, is still visible on the drawbridge tower. Otherwise the courtyard presents a delightful display of delicate arcades with a troop of decorative stone statues mustered for inspection.

As in Cangrande's day, the stronghold of Montegalda had been frequently contested in the Middle Ages although the contestants had usually appeared from nearer at hand: either Padua or Vicenza. Several documents refer to Montegalda's role in the great struggle between the free communes of northern Italy and the German Emperor, and claim that the castle was built by the Lombard League in 1176 to withstand the onslaught of Frederick Barbarossa. At that time the Lords of Montegalda were of the ancient Conti clan from whom the famous Maltraverso family descended. However, much of this history is uncorroborated speculation. Nonetheless, these names and dates serve to emphasize what is clear to any visitor who has mounted one of the towers at Montegalda and admired the extensive views over the surrounding country: that the lords of the castle enjoyed a considerable position of power and importance in the history of the Veneto and that their castle survives today as a spectacular monument to a prominent role in the past.

Villa Godi at Lonedo di Lugo, Vicenza. This is one of three country houses built by Palladio on a hilly site. Whereas La Rotonda was conceived as a hilltop leisure pavilion and Villa Barbaro was built on a gentle slope at Maser, Villa Godi's site is almost mountainous compared with the rest of the Veneto. In his article in the *Quattro Libri*, written almost thirty years after the villa was begun, Palladio describes the costs involved in building the approach roads. The villa was actually one of Palladio's earliest designs and bears the hallmarks of the apprenticeship he served prior to his first visit to Rome in 1541. When it was finished, with minor variations from the design shown in the *Quattro Libri* published in 1570, the exterior of the villa appeared to be more indebted to the architectural conventions of Palazzo Veneziana than to the ideas imitative of the classical style then in vogue in those Vicentine circles favoured by Giangiorgio Trissino, Palladio's commissioner and patron. Perhaps this discrepancy between the Godi villas and Palladio's subsequent drawings for country houses is due more to the tastes and the loyalty of his noble patrons, the brothers Gerolamo and Piero Godi of the wealthy Godi family of Vicenza. At the beginning of the sixteenth century, the city owed its importance to Enrico Antonio Godi (1451–1536), then renowned as "the new Demosthenes." From this it can be inferred that he had commissioned Palladio to build a villa which would look as classical as possible. But the reputation of this member of the Godi family stemmed not only from his creative capacities, but in particular from the loyalty which he showed to the Republic during the dark days of the League of Cambrai when many of the local nobles sided with the Emperor Maximilian. The Godi were completely loyal to the Republic and Enrico Godi was one of the ten noblemen from Vicenza appointed to give voice to the renewed allegiance to the Doge, Leonardo Loredan after the recapture of Padua. One of the Godi family's palaces in Vicenza was located in the district of San Vito near Palladio's own house. The villa at Lonedo was built on a terrace in the hills overlooking the River Astico and Palladio mentions that the *piano nobile* was more than thirteen feet above ground level. This would seem to follow the practise in urban houses of locating the main rooms in the house on the first floor, above the ground floor. The opening of the three arches in the center of the façade at this level corresponds in fact to the long room which runs the full length of the villa like the *portego* of a Venetian palace; this would seem to be another minor element borrowed from conventional urban architecture. The roof cornices, which could have projected further to create a more impressive effect, are limited to the dimensions which, in Venice at least, were ordered by public decree to avoid cornices overshadowing the narrow streets. When he published the *Quattro Libri* in 1570, Palladio seemed troubled by the lack of classical sophistication and added a disproportionately high central section to the villa, the only apparent purpose of which was to display the Godi coat-of-arms and to accommodate an exquisitely classical triangular tympanum. In contrast with the exterior of the Villa Godi, which was without classical ornamentation when it was finished, the interior was elaborately decorated and the villa is now famous for its spectacular cycle of frescoes by Gualtiero Padovano (?–1560), Battista del Moro (1514–75), and above all Giambattista Zelotti (1526–78). Gualtiero's frescoes most likely formed part of the original decorations executed in 1540, whereas Zelotti, unquestionably the better painter, did not work at Lonedo until fifteen years later. Gualtiero's Room of the Caesars and his Room of Triumphs are masterpieces of architectural and decorative motifs in which the painter has used an elaborate *trompe l'œil* technique.

Zelotti's *trompe l'œil* in the main hall, with hanging garlands and cornices, contain large guilded scrolls surrounding scenes from classical mythology, as well as vast tableaux portraying scenes from the life of Alexander the Great, a favourite subject in the houses of the Vicentine nobility since large numbers of their ancestors had followed military careers in the north of Italy.

Villa da Porto Colleoni, Thiene. There has always been a certain amount of confusion about how to describe the great fifteenth-century Gothic country house that today belongs to the Thiene family. The earliest documents refer to it as the Castello di Santa Marta although recent scholarly opinion denies it any past function as a fortress or castle. The absence of a moat or defensive ditch around the outer walls of the property has led to general agreement on this point, although some students claim that the present building has engulfed an earlier structure that might have been a castle. But critical opinion generally agrees that the most castle-like embellishments – the two towers with their swallow-tail merlons, or even the battlements outlined in relief under the roof-line on all four sides of the central block – are purely ornamental, reflecting a kind of latent nostalgia for feudal times. Today the building is most frequently referred to as the Villa da Porto Colleoni, after the well-known Vicentine family who inhabited it during the fifteenth century and were joined through marriage with the Colleoni family of Bergamo, whose most noted member, Bartolomeo, was one of the Venetian Republic's most successful *condottieri*. It is as a palace that its architecture should be understood, deriving as it does from the twelfth- and thirteenth-century palaces built in Venice in the Veneto-Byzantine style. The sources and characteristics of this derivation have already been discussed in the introduction yet, however the building may be described, it survives as the sole example of the source from which all Veneto villa architecture originated. In addition, certain elements contribute to a decorative and architectural assemblage of the highest quality, in particular such details as the five-light *portego* windows, framed with exquisitely carved dentil moulding, separated by graceful slender marble columns capped with foliate capitals, yet linked by a finely wrought marble balustrade. Another fifteenth-century Gothic element is to be found inside the building on the ground floor, where one of the lateral rooms was heated by an unusual fireplace with a deep semicircular mantelpiece and a tall rounded hood. The ornamental intention of these details, again more suited to a palace than to a villa of the fifteenth century, is also reflected in the splendidly carved and painted beams of the room. Today the intricate late Gothic patterns of this painting and even the extraordinary outlines of the fireplace are completely overwhelmed by the sixteenth-century fresco decoration of virtually every principal reception room in the house.

These frescoes, which attracted the attention of Giorgio Vasari among others, are one of the great treasures of Veneto fresco work, particularly those of the ground-floor "Camerone". They were executed by Veronese's colleague from Verona, Giambattista Zelotti (1526–78), and the slightly younger Vicentine artist, Giovanni Antonio Fasolo (1530–72). The scene representing the *Banquet of Anthony and Cleopatra* has been recognized as Fasolo's masterpiece while the individual gods and goddesses have been attributed to Zelotti. The *trompe l'œil* architecture framing each scene reaches from the floor to a splendid garland-hung frieze frescoed under the beams, creating a deeply receding perspective for the over life-size actors in these colourful tableaux.

The theatrical splendour of the interiors at Thiene are matched by one other building on the property. The early eighteenth-century stables are so splendid that they have been attributed to Francesco Muttoni (1648–1747) responsible for the exuberant design of several Baroque churches in Vicenza. The fine stalls recall the elaborate equestrian artifice characteristic of the *haute école* that was so popular in the seventeenth and eighteenth century. Aristocrats of every European country, as well as the commanding officers of the armies of the day, had their portraits painted, mounted on fine stallions that today could only be found among the Lipizzaners of Vienna, but which were then to be found in every noble stable.

The **Villa Della Torre** at Fumane is undoubtedly one of the most original villas in the Veneto. It was built during the first half of the sixteenth century for a member of the Della Torre family of Verona. The site they chose for their house was in the Valpolicella, the hilly river valley near Verona, famous for its vineyards. The Della Torre family of Verona, like the Serego and the Guarienti, had acquired fame and vast fortunes from their prowess as military commanders. From knights in the service of the Della Scala lords of medieval Verona, they had become the mercenary commanders or *condottieri* of the Serenissima's armies on the mainland. Their *condotta* or contract with the Republic was a source of considerable wealth, as was the immense booty they frequently claimed from victorious campaigns. These *condottieri* often sought to perpetuate their fame in monuments and works of art to a degree that made them, together with better-known colleagues such as the Sforza of Milan, the Gonzaga of Mantua or the Montefeltro of Urbino, among the most important patrons of Renaissance Italy. Given the taste of the times and, in Verona, the Roman ancestry of many of these families, it is not surprising that *condottieri* patronage of the arts had a strongly classical bias. Nowhere is this more evident than in the Villa Della Torre at Fumane.

However, for all its importance as a villa built along classical lines, nothing is known for certain about its architect. Credit for the design is often given to one or other of the two most important architects active in this part of the world during the first half of the sixteenth century: Michele Sanmicheli (1484–1559), who was well known for his work on palaces, villas and on the reconstruction of Verona's fortification, as well as for the design of the great classical-style gateways cut through the massive bastions and ornamented with the rusticated stonework derived from the civic engineering of classical antiquity; the other probable candidate is the slightly younger Giulio Romano (1499–1546), who had come to the Veneto from Rome to build a great suburban villa for the Gonzagas at Mantua. Romano is generally considered responsible for the popularity of heavy stone rustication as a decorative and architectural element; for all the Mannerist exuberance of its detail, his Palazzo del Te does resemble the Villa Della Torre in its conception as a low building constructed around a courtyard in imitation of the villas described by classical authors.

The originality of the Villa Della Torre lies in the way in which it turns inward to its courtyard, exactly as the classical villa was supposed to be organized around its peristyle and atria. In keeping with these villas, the courtyard at Fumane was planned with a surrounding colonnade, although each column is executed in that most extravagant of Mannerist architectural conceits – rusticated stone, that is, stone cut in such a way as to look natural. It seems that the Mannerist taste for the bizarre also dominated the interior, although most of the frescoes and stuccowork decoration survive only in fragments. Several of the spectacular fireplaces are still intact however. They resemble monstrous masks with grimacing features and gigantic roaring jaws, the fires laid in their mouths. One of these extraordinary creations, less grotesque than the others, recalls the lion's head helmet worn by Hercules in ancient legends and so often repeated in the elaborate ceremonial armour created for the *condottieri* and princes of Renaissance Italy.

The **Villa Serego** at Santa Sofia di San Pietro near Verona is one of the most puzzling of Palladio's unfinished villas. A great many of the buildings he designed were never completed according to his intentions and, as already mentioned, even the most complete often differ from the plans published by Palladio in 1570 in his *Quattro Libri*. The great palaces of Vicenza and many of Palladio's villas suffered this fate because of the terrible monetary inflation and crop failures that afflicted the Veneto at just about the time his treatise appeared in print. Although the unfinished state of the Villa Serego may have been the result of other considerations, Palladio's original design for the house presents almost as many unanswered questions as the actual state of the building today.

The Villa Serego was probably already under construction by the middle of the sixteenth century. It may well be the lavish use of stone – and this was Palladio's only essay in this costly and time-consuming material – that ultimately determined the villa's fate. Judging from Palladio's published plan the completed building would certainly have been immense. The present gigantic U-shaped wing represents about a quarter or less of the entire project. Palladio planned what was essentially an H-shaped structure. The lower projections were to be the building's *barchesse*, with the principal entrance through the cross bar of the H. The upper projections were to have been closed across the top with a simple wall, making this area an enclosed courtyard. As it exists today the villa represents only the left-hand half of this enclosed courtyard. In spite of the fact that it is only a fragment of the original plan, the architecture of this section is tremendously impressive. The magnificent cornice is supported by a fantastic order of Ionic columns whose long rusticated shafts rise through the two storeys of the building. The villa's apartments are situated deep in the shadows of the loggia behind this colonnade; a fine stone balustrade marks the level of the upper floor and underlines the visually unifying function of the cornice above. Palladio's project envisaged another identical wing facing this one to complete the enclosed and arcaded courtyard. The adjacent open-ended courtyard – the lower projections of the H shape of the villa – with its *barchesse* was also to be lined with a colonnade finished in the rusticated style that Palladio may have borrowed from Giulio Romano (1499–1546). Romano had brought this motif with him from the papal court at Rome when he came to build a great classical-style suburban villa, embellished with the latest Mannerist-style decoration, for the Gonzaga marquess of Mantua. Romano had also designed a rusticated gateway for Vicenza and Palladio is known to have used this model for his Palazzo Thiene.

Apart from Palladio's undisputed borrowing from Romano, scholars have completely overlooked the similarity in plan between the Gonzaga's villa and that designed for the Serego. Both the Serego and the Gonzaga families belonged to the proud, yet little studied or understood tradition of the *condottieri* as patron of the arts. Palladio's plan is a reminder that classical and Roman features were hallmarks of this tradition. The Villa Serego was unlike any villa subsequently designed by Palladio and indeed, both his probable borrowing from Romano and the fact that after the early villas (such as the Villa Pisani at Bagnolo) he hardly ever used full Roman rustication again, has led some to assume that his plans for Santa Sofia came very early in his career – indeed only shortly after his first trip to Rome in 1541. Be that as it may, the Roman inspiration behind the villa is evident from the fact that Palladio intended the central architectural focus to be found not in a temple front façade, as became typical of his later designs, but in the great courtyard. Palladio knew from his study of Vitruvius and other ancient authors that the courtyard was the center of a Roman house, and in the palaces he was building in Vicenza, especially in the heavily rusticated Palazzo Thiene, he made the courtyard the most important architectural and decorative feature.

Villa Allegri Arvedi, Cuzzano di Grezzana. The villas built near Verona are a restatement in slightly different terms of the Veneto villas that have been examined so far in this selection. First of all, they were usually built for families of the local nobility and not for Venetians or great princes of the church. The nobility of Verona had its own traditions of Roman ancestry and did not need the influence of papal Rome to indulge themselves in a revival of classical antiquity. These villas were also considerably enriched by their setting in vine-covered hills on river valleys or on the wooded shores of lakes, such as Garda, which provided a splendid backdrop to fine architecture realized with considerably more stone embellishment than the villas of Padua, Vicenza or Treviso.

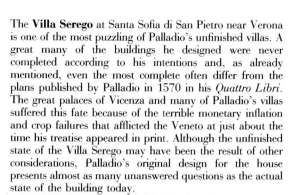

The Villa Allegri enjoys a particularly beautiful position in the Val Pantena, the valley of one of the River Adige's many tributaries that flow south to join the main river at Verona. The Lessini mountains open out into several such valleys, of which the Valpolicella is perhaps the best known. Neighbouring valleys such as the Val Pantena may be less famous, but they enjoy similar advantages for vine-growing. The Villa Allegri at Cuzzano di Grezzana is surrounded by vineyards and lies in all its magnificence against a hilly backdrop. The main block of the villa was built on the site of an older building, but its splendid façade and outbuildings were designed in the late sixteenth century by Giovanni Battista Bianchi (1520–1600). Its remarkably long façade extends through thirteen bays, without the benefit of the *barchessa* wings traditional in lowland farm villas. Nevertheless, Bianchi gives the building a central focus using elements borrowed from classical antiquity. However, the half columns are not arranged like a temple portico, but rather in the kind of blind arcading more often found in the architecture of mainland town palaces. The rooftop balustrade with its ornamental statuary also derives from the conventions of sixteenth-century urban architecture. These balustrades are continued on a lower level with the long wings that extend to the villa's handsome dovecote towers. These two tall square structures provide the terminal accents to an exceptionally long architectural composition which embraces the formal garden parterres planted in front of the house during the seventeenth century.

The villa's imposing façade has a certain theatrical quality that is reflected in the building's interior, where a splendid series of later frescoes by Lodovico Dorigny (1654–1742) suggests the continuing high standard of artistic patronage at the Villa Allegri. Dorigny's gesticulating figures are set in a fresco framework of the most impressive complexity. The plunging *trompe l'œil* perspectives are so elaborate and overwhelming that the name of the master stage designer Francesco Bibbiena (1659–1739) has been suggested as the author of the tour de force of fresco work preserved in the main hall of the villa.

The theatrical qualities of the property were further enhanced by the chapel, built in Baroque style in the courtyard behind the house. Reached by an elaborate double staircase the building commemorates a visit made by Carlo Borromeo, the sixteenth-century cardinal archbishop of Milan who was canonized in 1610.

The **Villa Badoer** at Fratta Polesine is one of the most beautiful of all Palladio's farm villas, yet its location in the marshy Polesine plains of the Po valley makes it the southernmost and the least known of his many masterpieces. In spite of its apparently remote situation Palladio was sufficiently impressed by the property's historical associations to summarize them in his article in the *Quattro Libri*. The village of Fratta lies on a tributary of the Adige, one of the Veneto's most important rivers: visitors are often frustrated because the high banks, which were constructed to prevent the flooding endemic in these lowlands, block their view of the villa. The villa itself was built for Francesco Badoer in 1556 on the site of an ancient castle, but had to be raised high above the damp marshy ground. Of course this practical provision perfectly suited Palladio's aesthetic convictions, because he knew that the ancient Romans required the portico of a temple to be raised and reached by a magnificent staircase. He also believed that adding a temple front portico to a Veneto farmhouse accurately reflected the external appearance of country houses or villas built in classical antiquity.

The Villa Badoer perfectly reflects the Roman virtue of *gravitas* and the ennobling nature of agricultural life as described by Latin writers. Palladio designed the villa's farm outbuildings as an integral part of the patrician residence. However, because of the restricted site, which was closed in by the river banks and by an ancient road, the *barchesse* could not be attached to the main block of the building, as was traditional in Veneto farmhouse design. Instead the *barchesse* were set along the edges of the site, at right angles to the house and some distance from it. Palladio always equated the arcaded façade of the traditional Veneto *barchessa* with the portico of classical antiquity and in his writings on the subject insists that this element be included in farm villa design. At the Villa Badoer he therefore borrowed the *barchessa's* traditional arcading and turned it into a proper classical portico, curving out from the villa's façade to reach the outlying farm buildings. He planned a great sweeping hemicycle of twenty-two columns that would embrace the entire forecourt of the property. Only a little over half of this wonderful colonnade was constructed according to the plan published in the *Quattro Libri*. However, a careful glance at the width of the site is sufficient to demonstrate that such a colonnade could never have been carried out according to the *Quattro Libri* and we have yet another example of Palladio embellishing his plans for the sake of the appearance of his book.

A similar consideration might explain why the large rear portico or the meandering garden walls were never built. All these elements make Palladio's plan a handsome piece of woodcut design, but correspond neither to reality nor to the practical considerations that so concerned him. This tendency to make the plates and plans in the *Quattro Libri* more elaborate undoubtedly explains the presence of so many ornamental statues depicted on the pediments of villas, when in reality virtually none were made for these façades in the sixteenth century. The interior of the Villa Badoer is as fine as any designed by Palladio and is similar in plan to that at Pojana. Palladio makes special mention of the Villa Badoer's fresco decoration, as he did for Pojana, in the *Quattro Libri*. His scrupulousness in this and other similar instances is a clear indication that, for all the classical simplicity of his architecture, Palladio's taste, and that of his patrons, in interior decoration was of the most lavish and ornate late-sixteenth century kind.

Bibliography

ACKERMAN J. S., *Palladio*, Harmondsworth, 1966.

— *Palladio's Villas*, New York, 1967.

ARGAN G. C., *Palladio e palladianesimo*, Vicenza, 1980.

AZZI VISENTINI M., *L'orto botanico di Padova e il giardino del Rinascimento*, Milan, 1984.

BAGATTI VALSECCHI P. F. - LANGÈ S., *La villa*, in *Storia dell'arte italiana*, 11: *Forme e modelli*, Turin, 1982, pp. 363-456.

BALDAN A., *Storia della Riviera del Brenta*, vol. 3, Vicenza, 1980-81.

BARBIERI F., *Vincenzo Scamozzi*, Vicenza, 1952.

— *Illuministi e Neoclassici a Vicenza*, Vicenza, 1972.

— and MENATO G., *Pietra di Vicenza*, Vicenza, 1970.

BARBIERI G., *Andrea Palladio e la cultura veneta del Rinascimento*, Rome, 1983.

BASSO U., *Cronaca di Maser, delle sue chiese e della villa palladiana dei Barbaro*, Montebelluna, 1968.

BERTOTTI SCAMOZZI O., *Le fabbriche e i disegni di Andrea Palladio*, vol. 1, Vicenza, 1776.

BLUNT A., *Le teorie artistiche in Italia dal Rinascimento al Manierismo*, Turin, 1966.

BORDIGNON FAVERO G. P., *La villa Emo di Fanzolo*, Vicenza, 1970.

BRAUDEL F., *La vita economica di Venezia nel secolo XVI*, in *La civiltà veneziana del Rinascimento*, Florence, 1958, pp. 81-102.

BRUNELLI B. - CALLEGARI A., *Ville del Brenta e degli Euganei*, Milan, 1930-31.

BRUNO G., *La riviera del Brenta. Le stagioni del tempo*, Cittadella di Padova, 1982.

CANOVA A., *Ville del Polesine*, Rovigo, 1971.

— *Le ville del Palladio*, Treviso, 1985.

— *Invito a Palladio*, Milan, 1980.

CEVESE R., *Ville della provincia di Vicenza*, vol. 2, Milan, 1971.

COZZI G., *Ambiente veneziano e ambiente veneto*, in *L'uomo e il suo ambiente*, Florence 1973. pp. 93-146.

— *Ambiente veneziano, ambiente veneto, governanti e governati nel Dominio di qua dal Mincio nei secoli XV-XVIII*, in *Storia della cultura veneta*, 4: *Il Seicento*, Vicenza, 1984, t. II, pp. 495-539.

CROSATO L., *Gli affreschi nelle ville venete del Cinquecento*, Treviso, 1962.

FIOCCO G., *Alvise Cornaro: il suo tempo e le sue opere*, Venice, 1964.

FORSSMAN E., *Palladios Lehrgebäude*, Stockholm-Göteborg-Uppsala, 1964.

GOLZIO V., *Seicento e Settecento*, Turin, 1950.

GUIOTTO M., *Monumentalità della riviera del Brenta. Itinerario storico-artistico dalla laguna di Venezia a Padova*, Padua, 1983.

IVANOFF N., *Palladio*, Milan, 1967.

KOLB C. J., *New Evidence for Villa Pisani at Montagnana*, in *Interpretazioni Veneziane*, Venice, 1984, pp. 227-239.

KOLB LEWIS C., *The Villa Giustinian at Roncade*, New York-London, 1977.

KUBELIK M., *Die Villa im Veneto. Zur typologischen Entwicklung im Quattrocento*, vol. 2, Munich, 1977.

MAZZARIOL G. and PIGNATTI T., *La pianta prospettica di Venezia del 1500 disegnata da Jacopo de' Barbari*, Venice, 1963.

MAZZOTTI G., *Ville Venete*, Rome, 1963.

MOLMENTI P., *La storia di Venezia nella vita privata dalle origini alla caduta della Repubblica*, vol. 3, Bergamo, 1927-1929.

MOMETTO P., *La vita in villa*, in *Storia della cultura veneta*, 5: *Il Settecento*, Vicenza, 1985, t. II, pp. 607-629.

MURARO M., *Palladio et l'urbanisme vénetien*, in *L'urbanisme de Paris et l'Europe: 1600-1680* (edited by P. Francastel), Paris, 1969, pp. 211-217.

— *Civiltà delle ville venete*, Udine, 1986.

— *Il Veneto nel Cinquecento* (in reply to G. Spini); *Fra' Giocondo da Verona e l'arte fiorentina*, in *Florence and Venice: Comparison and Relation*, II: *Cinquecento*, Florence, pp. 211-214, 337-339.

PALLADIO A., *I Quattro Libri dell'Architettura*, Venice, 1570 (Milan, 1951); trans. The Architecture of Palladio; in four books, London, 1721.

PRECERUTTI GARBERI M., *Affreschi settecenteschi delle Ville Venete*, Milan, 1968.

PUPPI L., *Palladio*, Florence, 1966.

— *Michele Sanmicheli archetto di Verona*, Padua, 1971.

— *La Villa Badoer di Fratta Polesine*, Vicenza, 1972.

— *Andrea Palladio*, vol. 2, Milan, 1973.

— *The Villa Garden of the Veneto from the Fifteenth to the Eighteenth Century*, in *The Italian Garden* (edited by D. Coffin), Washington, D.C., 1972, pp. 83-114.

RIGON F., *Palladio*, Bologna, 1980.

ROMANO R., *La storia economica. Dal secolo XIV al Settecento*, in *Storia d'Italia*, 2: *Dalla caduta dell'Impero romano al secolo XVIII*, Turin, 1974, t. II, pp. 1813-1931.

RUMOR S., *Storia breve degli Emo*, Vicenza, 1910.

RUPPRECHT B., *Villa. Zur Geschichte eines Ideals*, in *Probleme der Kunstwissenschaft*, vol. II, Berlin, 1966, pp. 120 ff.

RUSSEL ROOP G., *Villas and Palaces of Andrea Palladio*, Milan, 1968.

SANSOVINO F., *Venetia, città nobilissima et singolare descritta in XIII Libri*, Venice, 1581.

SCAMOZZI V., *Discorsi sopra le antichità di Roma*, Venice, 1583.

— *L'idea dell'architettura universale*, Venice, 1646.

SCARPARI G., *Le ville venete*, Rome, 1980.

SCHULZ J., *Venetian Painted Ceilings*, Berkeley-Los Angeles, 1968.

— *Jacopo de' Barbari's View of Venice: Map marking, City Views, and Moralized Geography Before 1500*, LX, pp. 425-474.

SEMENZATO C., *La scultura veneta del Sei e del Settecento*, Venice, 1966.

— *La Rotonda*, Vicenza, 1968.

— *Le ville del Polesine*, Vicenza, 1975.

SPEZZATI G., *Le ville venete della riviera del Brenta*, Dolo, 1976.

TAFURI M., *L'architettura del Manierismo nel Cinquecento europeo*, Rome, 1966.

— *Jacopo Sanzovino e l'architettura del '500 a Venezia*, Padua, 1969.

— *Venezia e il Rinascimento. Religione, scienza, architettura*, Turin, 1985.

VENTURA A., *Nobiltà e popolo nella società veneta del '400 e '500*, Bari, 1964.

Various authors, *Gli affreschi delle ville venete dal Seicento all'Ottocento*, vol. 2, Venice, 1978.

— *Palladio, Veronese e Vittoria a Maser*, Milan, 1960.

— *Vicenza illustrata*, Vicenza, 1976.

— *Palladio e Venezia*, edited by L. Puppi, Florence, 1982.

WITTKOWER R., *Architectural Principles in the Age of Humanism*, London, 1949.

ZORZI G. G., *Le Opere Pubbliche e i Palazzi privati di Andrea Palladio*, Venice, 1964.

— *Le chiese e i ponti di Andrea Palladio*, Venice, 1966.

— *Le ville e i teatri di Andrea Palladio*, Venice, 1969.